Movie
and
Videotape
Special
Effects

Also by Emil E. Brodbeck:

Handbook of Basic Motion Picture Techniques
(Amphoto, 1966)

Movie
and
Videotape
Special
Effects

Emil E. Brodbeck

Chilton Book Company
Philadelphia   New York   London

To Richard,
able assistant and the kind of young
man a father is proud to call "son"

Preface

This book is intended to be the best possible beginning manual for the area of special-effect work in 8mm and 16mm motion picture, videotape, and still photography. In researching extensively all types of material and ideas — and that means actually trying them out — I came upon much that was so advanced it would discourage all but those who were so experienced in photography that they would not need the information in the first place. Other information proved to be untested theory put forth by very competent cameramen who, understandably, had never actually used those theories in their own work. Many ideas for creating special effects were either too involved or, when simple, resulted in effects far too inferior to consider encouraging you to waste time attempting them.

While working on this book, I tried for myself under normal home conditions, most of the ideas I discuss, which means the results may be successfully accomplished by almost anyone in a basement, playroom, or low-budget studio. Other, outdoor effects may be achieved by simple techniques, without an expensive entourage of experts milling about.

While this book is a key to many things, it does not open the whole house, room, or even an entire closet of any particular area of possibilities. In each case it is the master key to many doors leading to endless fun, practical accomplishment, creativity, and a large measure of professionalism. But don't be scared off by the word "professionalism." It simply means that this book can show you how to do many things the easiest and best possible way.

*　　　*　　　*

In the realm of acknowledgments, I wish to thank the following companies for permission to reproduce their materials: Ampex Corp. for Figs. 10-1, 10-2, 10-3, and 10-4; Eastman Kodak Co. for Figs. 7-2, 7-3, 8-1, and 8-2, and for the discussion of close-up lenses on pp. 144-147; L & L Eastern Effects, Division of Berkey Video Services, Inc., (New York) for Fig. 1-1a; and UneCo, Inc. (Bellevue, Neb.) for Fig. 6-9.

In addition, I wish to express my profound gratitude to the following individuals — as well as to those who are not included for reasons of space or my faulty memory — for their sincere cooperation in helping me assemble essential information for this book: Carter G. Elliot, Ampex Corp.; Bruce S. Odom, Al Lindfors, and Roy Fehmel, Bell & Howell Corp.; Larry Lippman, Berkey Video Services, Inc.; John Flory, R. E. McMurtrie, Hank J. Kaska, Tom Levy, and J. E. Groff, Eastman Kodak Co.; Ed Nowak, Commercial Photographer; Fred

Onderka, Ernst Wildi, Paillard, Inc. (distributors of Bolex equipment); Robert W. Lawrence, Piolite Plastics Co.; Bill Safran, Willoughby-Peerless Camera Stores (New York); J. Goldberg, Samigon Corporation; Al Gordon, Sylvania Electric Products; Donald H. Ortiz, UneCo, Inc.; Victor Solow, Solow Productions; Harvey Hament, Roy Creveling, Slide-O-Chrome; A. E. Osolin, Weston Instruments, Inc.; Hollywood Valley Film Laboratories, Inc.; and Sparta Photo Service (New York).

E. E. B.

Contents

1

The Wide Range of Special Effects: "Opticals" and the Matte Box

One of the most interesting and virtually unlimited areas in the realm of motion-picture and videotape special effects is that of "opticals." So-called because in professional film production they are accomplished by optical printing machines, opticals include (1) the conventional sort of transitions such as fade-outs (where the end of a scene is progressively darkened until it blacks out), fade-ins (where the screen starts out black and the scene gradually becomes more distinct), dissolves (where one scene dissolves into the next — actually a fade-in superimposed on a fade-out), and wipes (where, for instance, a black area travels across the screen from one side to another, gradually "wiping" out the scene and leaving the screen black); (2) effects the audience is unaware of, such as combining, in the final projected image, actors shot in a studio with a background shot on location; and (3) many other effects, such as freeze frame (where action is frozen), reverse action, superimposed titles, and so forth. Effects of this kind are often the icing on the cake, that extra window dressing, the something extra that makes your photographic effort better than average and gives it that professional touch. While many of these effects can be produced in the camera, the laboratory approach is admittedly more scientific and the results from a good lab are most professional. You, too, can use such labs. I strongly advise that you visit one; they are an education in themselves.

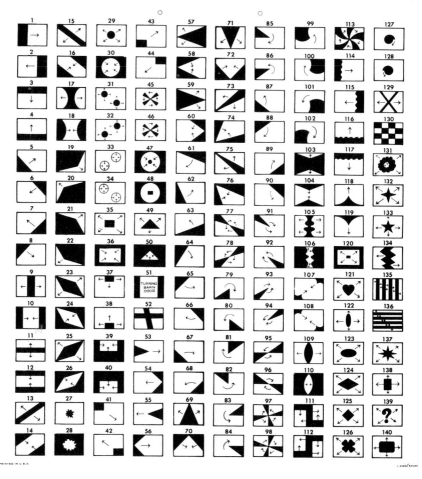

Fig. 1-1a

Before exploring how to achieve special effects in the camera, then, let us see how the film laboratory produces them.

Special Effects Laboratories

Most labs can give you all kinds of special effects if you supply them with motion-picture scenes on 35mm or 16mm film. If you normally work in regular 8mm or Super 8mm and wish to have a lab make special effects for you, my advice is to borrow or rent a 16mm camera and shoot all the scenes in which you would want special effects on 16mm. The lab can make the effects you desire and reduce them to either 8mm or Super 8mm, and you can later splice the completed effect scenes in with your other film. Also explore the possibility of shooting still slides and having special effect movie scenes made from them.

You will find optical printing labs in areas in which professional motion-picture studios and television stations are located; for instance, the New York, Chicago, and Los Angeles areas. Two labs that sent me information promptly when I was doing research for this book were L & L Eastern Effects, 219 E. 44th St., New York, N. Y. 10017 (extensive special effect work) and Hollywood Valley Film Laboratories, 2704 W. Olive, Burbank, Calif. 91505 (they can make effects during reduction printing from 35mm or 16mm to Super 8mm).

Just to give you an idea of the vast number of effects possible in one of these labs, reproduced here is L & L Eastern Effects' chart of 140 different wipes (Fig. 1-1a). The arrows indicate the direction of the movement in the effect. For example, the No. 1 wipe consists of more and more black moving to the right of the frame as the scene progresses so that the scene is wiped out from left to right. Number 2 wipes out the scene from right to left. Number 15 would start at the center and wipe out the scene diagonally to upper right and lower left simultaneously.

Listed under Eastern's "Optical Special Effects" are besides wipes, dissolves, and fades, these other effects: optical straight-line zoom, optical zoom with pans, flip, melt or ripple effect, freeze frame, reverse action, speed-up or slow-down action, superimposed titles with drop shadow, hidden split device, 360-degree spin camera, double exposure, translucent product effect, kaleidoscope, invisible split screen, regular split screen, spinning scene, halo or glow effect, skip framing, multiple framing, pan master, normal and high gamma, blue-screen process, red-screen process, infrared process, color cynexing from original color negative, insert and other matte work, color intermediate master (registered), and black-and-white prints registered for rotoscope. You will find other laboratories like this listed in such publications as *Photo Dealer*. When contacting these labs, I suggest that you take one step at a time. Ask direct, concise questions confined to what you actually want to accomplish at the time. This makes it possible for the lab, in turn, to give you a pertinent answer. Even if you do not wish to have a lab make any special effects for you, you really should become acquainted with at least one fine lab. You can always use them for duplicating film. Most professionals do not project their originals. They usually have a workprint made, which they edit and from which they then have master dupes made. Whether you go professional or not. it is a good idea to have some of your edited, most precious film duplicated so that you can project the dupe while you keep the "master" in a safe, cool place to prevent its getting scratched and dirty.

Fades

Some 16mm cameras and a few regular 8mm cameras allow you to run the film backwards (without exposing it) so that you can make lap dissolves and double exposures in the camera. However, the vast majority of movie cameras do not have this feature, and at this writing the new and rightfully popular Super

11

8mm cameras are cartridge-loaded and cannot be backed up. Since this is a basic book, it must deal with the problem of the majority of the cameramen who might read it; since the majority will not be able to back up their film, my job is to show you how to get around this limitation to produce special effects. One of the simplest substitutes for an in-camera dissolve is an in-camera fade. First you should understand why you might use such an effect. There will be many times when a change of scene will require proper transition in order to avert a startling or bumpy switch from one location to another, or from one period of time to another. In short, you need a connection between two sequences — a shot that would take the place of the old standby transitions (flipping pages of a calendar, turning hands of a clock). The fade provides that shot and avoids the need for explanation. Usually the fade employed for such a continuity link is really a fade-out in one scene and a fade-in in the next. The end of the leading scene grows darker, darker, darker — all the way to complete blackout. The head, or beginning, of the following scene should come from blackout, gradually lighting up, until finally the scene is properly exposed. (The length of the scene is calculated without the footage used for the effect.)

The easiest way to do this is just to turn the lens aperture gradually all the way down to its smallest opening while you are filming the end of the last scene in the sequence you wish to fade out. When you are set to shoot the following scene, you gradually open up the diaphragm of the camera, while it is running, until you reach the setting that will give correct exposure. When you reach the correct aperture, allow the camera to continue running long enough at that setting so that the audience will see a scene of normal length, all at the proper exposure. When you project the film, you will find that the last scene in the first sequence will grow gradually darker toward the end. Immediately after the screen goes completely dark, the fade-in at the beginning of the next scene will start, growing gradually lighter until it reaches the proper exposure. This simple device tells the audience that there has been a time lapse or shift of location between sequences, but without having to interject a transitional scene.

If your camera is completely automatic, you may create this effect by gradually dimming the light sources down beyond the capacity of the built-in meter to adjust to the light. When total darkness is reached, gradually bring the light sources, in the new scene, up out of total darkness to proper exposure level. Another way is to get an old shutter of the iris type with leaves that close in from a large circle to a minute one as you change aperture settings. The fade-out and fade-in can be done by closing down and opening up the leaf shutter. The shutter, mounted on a board of proper dimension and thickness, may be set either in front of or behind the opening of a matte box, which we shall discuss next.

The Matte Box

This brings us to the most invaluable accessory an amateur cameraman can own — the matte box. This is the poor man's Aladdin's Lamp, for general use and special effects in the simplest manner at lowest cost. While you could make

12

Fig. 1-1b

one out of an old bellows or view camera, I strongly suggest that you buy a good one. The matte box is a vital tool, and vital tools should be precisely built and capable of professional use. Several companies make matte boxes in various price brackets, but I recommend the Bolex matte box because it has the features I consider most necessary in such a device. They are: (1) grooved slide arrangements at both *front* and *rear* of the sliding bellows that allow glass or plastic slides, slide pictures, single movie frames, strips of frames suitably mounted, opal or ground glass, gelatine filters, other filters properly mounted, masks of all types to be inserted in either horizontal or vertical positions; (2) both front and rear ends of the matte box can be moved along a precisely calibrated scale that is part of a double rodlike setup designed to lock the front and rear ends in the desired position parallel to the film plane and lens (this alignment is necessary to avoid distortion), and (3) extension arms that can be put in place as long slides on the front of the matte box so that you can make wipes in the camera.

If you look at Fig. 1-1b, I think you will see what I am talking about. I am not suggesting, by any means, that the Bolex matte box is the only adequate one on the market. It does provide an example of the features you should consider minimum in such a device. Consult with your local camera dealer and the manufacturer of your own camera to see if they recommend any other make for your particular equipment. You can and should show them Fig. 1-1b and check out

Fig. 1-2

what you should have on the device as listed under (1), (2), and (3), above.

In Fig. 1-2, the cameraman is not looking through the viewfinder. This is a basic, easy-to-use Ampex Videotape TV camera, and the viewfinder lens is set off from the taking lens. The cameraman is looking around the camera to insert a binocular-type matte, or mask, and will watch the effect on his TV monitor (a TV set on which the picture he is shooting is simultaneously televised). He will keep the monitor positioned so he may use it as his viewfinder. The monitor shows the field of vision, depth of field, contrast, and so on instantly, a tremendous advantage. You can adjust the aperture, focus, and lighting, and see immediately what result is being received by the videotape. I constantly use my videotape setup to check special effects before putting them on film. Since the videotape is black-and-white and I shoot most of my motion pictures in color, there are differences, but you'd be surprised how much less film has to be shot in testing, especially in any case in which action or effect is a little out of the ordinary.

Adapting the Matte Box to Your Camera

I knew I would be using the matte box constantly with three of my cameras, and since the Bolex matte box is essentially designed to fit Bolex movie cameras, it would not attach properly to my cameras — a Bell & Howell Super 8mm

14

movie camera, a Canon Pellix 35mm still camera, and an Ampex TV Video-tape sound and visual tape recording camera. I was not concerned with my regular standard Bell & Howell 16mm professional equipment, because in 16mm, I can have all the special effects done by a lab.

Whether you buy a Bolex matte box or another make, it probably will not fit more than one of your cameras. I decided it was a waste of time to try to find any type of universal conversion bracket that would convert the matte box to different cameras. Instead, I went to a local ironworks. They had a scrap L-shaped bracket (shown painted white in the figures here) that just happened to be ideal. Even if an ironworks must make up such a piece for you, the charge could hardly be more than $2.50. First go to the ironworks and find out what the stock widths and lengths are in angle-iron girders from which they might have scrap. Then make a wood mock-up out of two pieces of 3/8-inch or 1/4-inch plywood with holes bored so that the bracket fits on your tripod and so that the matte box and cameras are held securely. Once you are sure this is correct, you can go to the ironworks and show them just what you want. I have included a sketch of the bracket I made up (Fig. 1-3a) so that, in case you have equipment with retaining holes and lenses set as mine are, you can just duplicate the bracket I made.

This bracket is painted white so that you can easily distinguish it from the tripod, camera, and matte box fittings as you study its construction. This same bracket is used atop my Quick-Set, Ampex (TV), and other tripods. I see no reason why it could not be used on any tripod. By boring the proper holes to attach the camera and the matte box of your choice, you could probably use this bracket in at least 80 per cent of the cases you would run across.

Figure 1-3b shows these items:

Fig. 1-3a

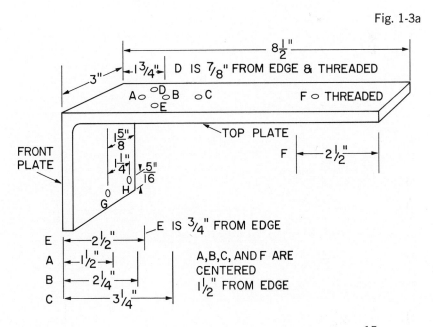

15

Fig. 1-3b

Fig. 1-3c

A file, needed to file down all burrs caused by drilling. File both sides of any hole and always drill the hole from the top down and from the outside of the bracket to the inside. Take care to have no raised areas between the matte box holding bracket and/or your camera and the bracket. Rough surfaces can damage the camera case and can cause misalignment.

Some taps and drills. Although I have shown more than one, I suggest you use only one tap — the proper one for making a threaded ¼-20 hole, which is the thread used on most tripod heads and camera receiving holes. (It is also a very common hardware thread.) I suggest that you only tap (thread) the hole or holes to fix the bracket securely to the tripod head. You will probably need two separate holes — one for your standard-size tripod and one for your light-weight tabletop tripod. The tabletop tripod should have the hole placed so that the weight of the bracket and all the equipment is directly over the center of the tripod. The standard heavy-duty tripod can carry weight that is a little off-center. The other holes that you will need to drill through the top of the white bracket are to hold the camera to it. Therefore, do not thread these, just make them large enough so that the retaining set bolt of the camera will slip through it snugly. You will have difficulty tightening the camera to the bracket if you thread the hole in the white bracket.

Some ¼-20 thread "eye," or wing, bolts if you cannot get the knurled, or round, thumb bolts usually used to secure cameras to tripods and into some carry cases. You will probably need some of different lengths because you may have to raise your camera to center it on the matte box openings (so that the lens will be centered in rear opening of box). I found that all I needed were two pieces of ¼-inch plywood, 3¾ inches long and 1-1/16 inches wide, with one hole, just a shade larger than ¼ inch, located 1½ inches from one end and equidistant from the sides. This hole is for the camera retaining bolt. In order to be certain that it is identically placed in both pieces of plywood, the pieces should be clamped together and the hole drilled through both at the same time. I do not use these ¼-inch shims when using my Super 8mm movie camera, but I use one under the videotape camera and two under the Canon Pellix. Both the movie camera and the 35mm Pellix can be loaded and operated without being removed from the bracket or tripod. Remember to make shims so that they will not interfere with the rewind release and camera-back locking device on the bottom of the 35mm still camera. If they are too large, they will cover up these devices, to which you must have access to reload without removing the camera. Also be careful to locate your bracket so all retaining bolts can easily be tightened without removing the bracket from the tripod head. Use nuts, washers, or other collars having a wide flat strong surface on the eye bolts and any other bolts so that when the bolt is securely tightened, the collar will allow you to turn the bolt tight without having the eye or other section chew up the underside of your bracket or catch in the hole and prevent your turning the bolt easily.

In Fig. 1-3c, you see the matte box receiver being bolted securely onto the downward-turned front face of the base of the L-shaped white bracket. Holes were drilled to accept these bolts snugly. Nuts and lock washers were used on the inside of the white bracket (after the bolts went through the black slide-retaining receiver and the white bracket). This receiver must be very securely fastened

17

Fig. 1-4

so that it will hold the matte box exactly and rigidly parallel to the film plane and the camera lens. Your matte box should have a receiver like this because the whole matte box arrangement slides into the receiver and is locked into it when the thumb bolt in the matte box assembly is tightened into the hole between the two bolts that hold the receiver to the white bracket. Thus, to attach or remove the matte box, you slide on the matte box and tighten the thumb bolt or unloosen the thumb bolt and slide off the matte box. One simple locking or unlocking operation is all it takes.

Masks

In Fig. 1-4, there are two different sizes of mattes, or masks, six masks in each size: three blank (solid); one binocular; one keyhole; and one heart. The blanks may be cut out to any shape design you wish or used as is to render sections of your film blank. Bolex provides at least this number of masks plus some acetate and glass slides with their matte box; no doubt other matte box manufacturers also supply such basic masks.

The six smaller masks are the right size to fit in the smaller matte box opening (the one closest to the camera lens). The larger masks fit the slides at the opposite (larger) ends. If you wish to cut out additional masks, I suggest black

Fig. 1-5a

Fig. 1-5a

Fig. 1-5b

construction paper of the type used for photo album pages. It is fairly rigid but can be cut easily. For additional rigidity, the cut mask can be mounted on a glass plate, between two pieces of acetate, or in a cardboard frame such as is used to hold 35mm slides.

I prefer to work with the effect mask in the larger, forward opening so that the matte box bellows forms an excellent lens shade and the rear side of the mask (the side that faces the camera lens) is inside the bellows. Even under the most adverse light conditions, the side of the mask facing the camera lens cannot pick up any reflection or develop any kind of halo on the rear side of the mask. Even black can form reflections if there is the slightest smoothness or shine to its surface. Though there will be times when you will want, perhaps even have, to use the smaller rear opening, usually using the larger one, which is further from the camera lens and closer to the point of focus, will make it possible to get the shape you wish, more clearly defined, around the subject area. Sometimes, of course, you want a vague outline. If you cannot obtain it by using the larger opening closer to the lens, you can change over to using the smaller bellows opening.

Figure 1-5a illustrates that if you shoot a scene through an effect mask such as this binocular one with your lens diaphragm set at its largest opening, you will see considerably more illumination and area and the outline of the mask will be more vague than if the lens is stopped down to a smaller aperture. Figure 1-5 shows what the 35mm Canon Pellix still camera sees through the $f/1.8$ opening. Figure 1-5b shows what the same camera in the same position but stopped down to $f/16$ will see. The point is that a larger opening shows more area within the mask and the mask outline is vague; whereas a smaller opening shows less area and the outline is clearer. Obviously, what is involved here is a difference in depth of field, the area in which objects are relatively sharp. Depth of field is increased by shorter focal length lenses, by smaller lens openings, and by further points of focus. Depth of field is decreased by longer focal length lenses, larger lens openings, and closer points of focus. If your camera enables you, be sure to check your scene before you shoot it at the aperture at which you will expose the scene. Also remember that a zoom lens has less depth of focus at the telephoto positions (because the lens has a longer focal length at these settings) than at its wide-angle or normal focal length settings.

If you do not have a camera that allows you to check focus and depth of field directly through the taking lens, I suggest that you film a series of actual tests (properly captioned at the beginning of each test). From these results, you can then make up a chart of the different coverages you will actually have at stops you might normally use. The differences shown in Figs. 1-5 and 1-6 are the ones that would exist with the normal lens in place on my 35mm film Canon Pellix. A standard lens for a 16mm camera and the normal lens on my Ampex TV camera are about 25mm, so you would have less difficulty with the 16mm than with 35mm. The standard lens for most 8mm and Super 8mm cameras is only 12.5 to 15mm (for some you can even get extreme wide-angle lenses of 10mm and 5.5mm), so even with the 12.5mm to 15mm lens or the zoom lens set at wide angle, you will have about half the problem with depth of field that you'd have with 16mm. Consequently, if you do not close down to more than $f/4.5$ or $f/5.6$ with an 8mm camera, you will not usually have too much diffi-

20

Fig. 1-6

culty using the viewfinder as is on such cameras as the Bell & Howell, which shows you exact size of field and exact placement of the subject through the taking lens although it does not show you depth of field. Focus and depth of field must be checked through a separate lens to one side of the taking lens.

A great advantage of the matte box used with masks is being able to mask out unwanted surroundings that you might otherwise be forced to include in your scene. Take, for example, a young child's birthday party. You need some regular long, medium, and other distance shots in order to keep your audience oriented. However, at many birthday parties some of the best scenes (serving the cake, etc.) take place in the kitchen, and it is often desirable to show as little of the background and overall area as possible.

In the series of shots shown in Fig. 1-6, we can see how the heart-shaped mask serves more than one purpose. Once we have the orientation long shot, the mask eliminated unnecessary and confusing background as well as a number of other children making a variety of grimaces and attempting to get their pictures taken. We were able to single out the object of our affections, quite appropriately in a heart, without the other children being offended or even realizing that our little culprit had the stage all to herself, while they — and all their antics — were completely masked out of the scene. You may feel this is pretty dirty pool, but it makes the task of the cameraman a lot easier and keeps everyone a lot happier while the scene is being shot. Also, when the film is projected, the audience will immediately accept the scene as cute and not resent the exclusion of the other children (some of which may be their own) from this particular scene. They will be quite happy if their children appear in the longer distance shots.

The technique of using such a mask is as follows: Once you have the subject framed within the mask and some footage rolled off at this position, you move in either by physically moving the camera up and sliding the heart mask closer to the camera lens before shooting the next scene or zooming in "through the heart" with a zoom lens. Either way, you should manipulate your equipment and accessories so that the audience has the feeling of being transported through the heart closer to the subject. Once this is done, you have a natural reason to make some extreme close-ups and capture those priceless moments of unique expression. You must always remember that there is no such thing as a really private "home movie." With little or no coaxing you will show your films to others, so, whether you are an amateur or a professional, use good taste and good sense. Whenever you pick up a camera, you might as well admit that you do it with the intention to record, instruct, and entertain, and that you are going to show your pictures to others. Others constitute a true audience, so *all* your pictures should be audience-worthy.

The Matte Box and Miniature Sets

Your professionalism, fun, and achievement with still, movie, videotape cameras — especially in the special effects department — can often be greatly enhanced through the use of miniature sets. The one shown in Fig. 1-7 is built on the underside of a standard tournament-size Ping-Pong table. Even in this

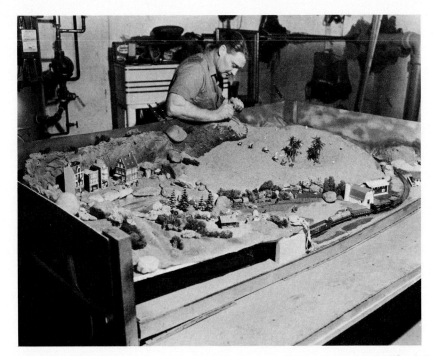

Fig. 1-7

Fig. 1-8

small area (about 4' x 8'), it was possible to build at least 4 different sets that could remain standing at the same time: (1) an old-fashioned seaport (with a cliff background); (2) a backwoods log-cabin area; (3) a farmland area with a railroad station, and (4) a desert area. Although not completely visible, an HO model railroad track layout completely encircles these sets.

The advantage of having your own sets is that you can work on them whenever the spirit moves you and alter them in any way you please. The sets, in addition to being used as scenes themselves, may be photographed (in still slides or movies) and projected onto a process screen as a background to other scenes. (More about this in Chapter V, on backgrounds.)

Before building your own sets, check around with your friends who are model railroaders, racers, airplane builders (with special attention to the railroaders), and see what gauge, or scale, their sets and models are. One of the most common is HO. It is wise to get all your figures, cars, trains, tractors, airplanes, and buildings as nearly as possible in the same, popular scale in order to afford yourself the widest interchangeability, as well as the opportunity to buy manufactured items. In this way there will be no problem in borrowing or buying props for your sets or in intermingling shots of friends' layouts with your own. This will allow you the greatest scope at lowest cost.

In this chapter we will concentrate mainly on the use of the matte box on miniature set scenes, since the effects are much the same when the masks are used for real-life scenes.

Figure 1-8 shows the matte box, white retaining bracket, and a tabletop tripod being used in conjunction with a 35mm Canon Pellix still camera with a 50mm lens. A tabletop tripod is vital to miniature set work as it enables you to place the camera close to one scene without materially upsetting the set. If you select such a tripod wisely, it can also serve many uses in the field. Try to buy one that places the camera about four feet above ground level when all the leg sections are fully extended. It should also have a crank-up center post so that fine adjustments can be made without moving the tripod legs. The head should be able to turn, tilt up and down, and tilt to at least one side. When the center post is fully cranked up to its highest point, there ought to be provision to raise the camera at least another 6 inches. When the tripod is fully contracted it should come to a height of only 12 to 15 inches above ground level. Such a tripod allows you to work at a level that makes sense in relation to the set. A tabletop tripod has many uses afield as well as indoors. It is handy in situations where weight and bulk must be kept to a minimum. When using a telephoto lens that is of extremely long focal length, the lens itself may be mounted on the tripod. It can also be used as a quick unipod (with legs all together when shooting zoom shots of action). Extreme low-angle shots also require its use.

The lighting in Fig. 1-8 is set to show the binocular mask and the setup of the tripod, camera, and matte box. It would be wrong for a shot of the scene itself. You will note that the cameraman loosened the thumb bolt at the front end of the matte box. With this set bolt loose he may, while looking in his camera viewfinder, adjust the mask to regulate how much of the scene will appear in the binoculars.

Suppose that you are shooting a desert scene as shown in Fig. 1-9a and some of the sand-colored retaining cloth shows. You may not wish to build up

Fig. 1-9a

Fig. 1-9b

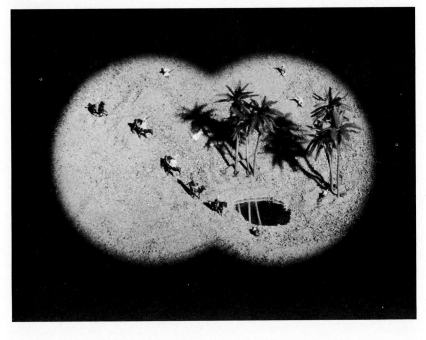

the sand further, but as it stands it does not give a realistic effect. You could raise the camera so that the angle of view would cut out the unwanted section. However, raising the camera at this close an angle foreshortens the figures and objects in the scene considerably and diminishes the significance of everything shown. In Fig. 1-9b, the binocular mask solves the problem. It confines audience view to less area and fewer figures so that everything remaining in the scene is more significant. When you are going to follow your long shot with such significant scenes as in Fig. 1-9b, aided by the binocular mask, you can get by with less footage in your long shot and a less effective overhead view. You have shifted the scene need in the long shot from a need for photographically detailed explanation to an introductory impression. Before the audience has a chance to try to look closely at details in the long shot, you cut from that scene and go into a closer shot in which the camera angle and distance are vastly superior for showing detail. To all except the trained eye, the inadequacies of the initial long shot, forced upon you by inadequacies of the set, will not be noticed. The perfect point at which to switch from the long shot to the more intimate scene is when the average audience has said to itself, "I wonder how some of those figures would look if I got a little closer?" But you shall have cut the shot too short if the thought is, "What the ——— was *that*?" No one can evaluate for you exactly how many feet long each scene should be, especially in the case of special effects, as each different scene, its subject content, and type of effect used are variables in each instance. For general rules, however, use the following table:

Length	Number of Feet in 16mm	Number of Feet in 8mm
Ultra-short	½ ft. or less	¼ ft. or less
Short	1	½
Medium	2	1
Long	4 or more	2 or more

Only experience will give you the feel of proper scene lengths, but these guides will start you on your way.

I must pause to issue a warning at this point! It is quite easy to get sloppy about your lighting when doing special effects. Whatever you do, do not let special effects spoil your picture-making techniques. Always use your other techniques to contribute to the effectiveness of your special effects. Lighting, in particular, can contribute much to both the beauty and the impact of an effect. The lighting in Figs. 1-9a and 1-9b is fine if the sun is supposed to be high in the sky, beating down on the desert, creating a hot, flat-looking scene. If, however, you wish to show a lapse of time, this should be shown by the lighting. A lower main light source giving longer shadows is called for "later in the day." Such lighting gives you a chance to create pictures with more texture, eliminates washing out bright areas such as sand, and gives more volume to everything in the scene.

Figure 1-10a is an example of what a low light source can do. It should be

Fig. 1-10a

Fig. 1-10b

noted that what makes texture is the ability of the camera to see enough of the shadow side of anything in the scene to outline lighter areas. You must achieve this without washing out the directly illuminated parts of the scene; carefully observe the effect as you move lights.

In Fig. 1-10b the binocular mask starts centering the audience's interest. For the next shot you can again discard the binoculars and move in to concentrate on small groups or on individual objects in the set.

If you are working with slides or still pictures, animation is no problem; in movies and videotaping it is.

In sets of this type, unless you wish to go to great expense, you'll have to use figures whose extremities cannot be moved; the limbs, head, hands, and feet will be statue-like, in permanently fixed positions. Figure movement must, therefore, be limited to moving the entire figure slightly between each frame. We will go into animation of such figures in more detail in Chapter 6. Right now let's see how we can use a special effect technique to circumvent this problem.

One of the most effective, but simplest solutions is to title or narrate your film (or tape) so that you actually use your problem to advantage and dramatically present the scenes, in which all figures are motionless, as carefully planned tableaux in which you have magically frozen time. This kind of subterfuge should become your stock in trade; that is, when you run headlong into an insurmountable obstacle, try to turn it to your advantage. When there is no way to eliminate a problem, use it, as though you meant for it to exist in the first place. You'll be amazed at how many times this can actually work well for you.

Let's say you want to prepare the audience for a live — that is, *real* — fishing scene. Figure 1-11a illustrates an ideal application of the *modus operandi* mentioned above, in which extremely professional-looking results have been achieved. In the title just preceding the long shot of the old-fashioned village, very interesting comment was made about the spear and net fishing, the rowboat, and two men, so that the audience's attention was immediately diverted from the village itself and all the small figures in it. Naturally, if you have sound-on-film, your narration would immediately deal with the rowboat and with the men fishing from it. By visual direction (or by sound direction, if you can provide it), your titles relegate the small village to the status of background. Let's see what this can accomplish for you in the matter of deception. Look intently at the two figures in the rowboat, just as your audience would if a title or narration had just directed their attention to this area. You will find that your eyes are immediately going to eliminate detail in the background by throwing the village into soft focus. Remember this characteristic of the human eye: it focuses on objects of its attention and throws peripheral objects out of focus.

This does not mean that you can overlook any opportunity to improve the reality of the scene, even in the background. Unless you are indicating that this is a tableau — a freeze-motion scene — move the figures in the background, as naturally as possible with the handicap of immobile limbs. The movement should be very slight from frame to frame. (More about this technique in the chapter on animation.) Meanwhile, do everything possible with the rowboat and the two figures in it to indicate more motion than is occurring in the background. If the deception is to work effectively, the audience must be more captivated with the two figures in the rowboat.

Fig. 1-11a

Fig. 1-11b

Having given the audience the opportunity to get an impression of the village in the soft-focus long shot, you can now put your real time-and-work-saver in place — the good old binocular mask — and really confine attention (Fig. 1-11b). Now, you only have to worry about animating two figures. If you wish to go to the trouble and expense you can carefully alter these figures so that limbs can be moved, or you can buy two figures for the rowboat that have movable limbs. This would be more important if you do not intend to switch to live figures. However, if you are going to switch to live figures, you must be sure that the real boat and figures are similar to the rowboat and the two statue-like figures in it. Everything in the scene should be the same type and color, right down to articles of clothing. This assumes, of course, that your intention is to present the village as a real one and the figures involved as live ones. With the idea of later switching to live actors in the rowboat, you show the two figurines in the boat carefully concentrating on scanning the water for prey and readying themselves (as well as they can without moving their limbs) by searching and standing poised for action. The boat is drifting away from shore during this sequence. At this point you can discard the binocular mask and move in for close-ups and extreme close-ups of the live action shots of the faces, hands on the net, the net going into the water, fish just below the surface, the spear-thrower poised for his thrust, the thrust, the spear entering the water, the catch, and so on. Since the audience only remembers accurately no more than one or two preceding scenes, by the time you move your camera back for a longer shot (in which the background will show) you need only a similar rocky shoreline. After such medium and long shots, you can move closer again for a shot of one of the men rowing and then a close-up of the oars as they dip into the water, the pail of fish, one man in the boat looking at his watch, then perhaps a shot of this man pointing to another possible fishing spot, and finally a little more rowing. At this point you would have almost complete freedom of choice of background when you move back for subsequent medium and long-distance shots. You would, of course, have to be careful not to be too nonchalant. You could not, for example, have the men row from one century of time to another or from a rural village background to a rip-roaring summer resort complete with high-powered motor craft trailing bikini-clad water-skiers.

I have spent considerable time on just two masks, but not because I think that you'll confine yourself to these two masks — or for that matter to masks alone — in your special effects. The important point is that there is finesse, there is technique, involved in the utilization of any special effect, and that the effect, if used without reason, meaning, and technique, is quite apt to be a dismal failure. By covering, in depth, how much technique can be employed around even the simple binocular-type mask, I'm sure that I have illustrated that the special effect accomplishes its purpose most completely and successfully when used as a natural fiber in the fabric of your pictorial story. While special effects should add color, interest, and logical continuity to the whole cloth of the story, they usually succeed best when used sparingly, or when its use seems logical (for example, a shot of racing horses through binoculars). The secret is that you must not rely on the effect alone, but must make the scene content as good in action, composition, lighting, etc., as possible so that the special effect becomes the servant of the scene, not the master of it.

Other Mask Effects

Because you may make as many kinds of masks as your imagination will allow, the matte box is a source of endless special effects. A silhouetted fence can be introduced in the foreground over any appropriate scene by cutting out a mask consisting of two parallel heavy strips crossed by two vertical posts. A combination of a title and a wipe may be made by using a title cell (a clear glass or acetate rectangle with title lettering on it) in combination with a wiping mask in the front section. A double wipe — two cardboard masks joined at center at the beginning of a scene, then opened up as the scene is being shot — is also a very professional-looking effect. Reverse this procedure and you can eliminate a scene by moving the cardboards together until they join at the center at the scene end. An arrow or other marker (for instance, an X) may be cut out and mounted on acetate or glass and may be put in the front frame so that it will be superimposed on a certain area of the scene being shot. A scene may appear to be shot through a window if you make a window-frame mask with black paper cross bars and mount this on glass or acetate. These are just a few possibilities.

The matte box may also be used for copying color slides and movie frames. If your camera cannot be focused close enough or if the focal length of your lens is too long, you will require extension tubes for such close work. Slides of major state and national parks, historic sites, museums, and so on can be bought in photo shops, in many drug stores, and even in the places themselves. If the weather or lighting conditions (especially inside some buildings and caverns) prohibit filming good motion pictures, you can either shoot the necessary shots with your still camera or buy them. Later you can copy the commercial slide or print as a movie scene. Consult your camera dealer and purchase the necessary extension tube (and any other auxiliary equipment necessary for your particular camera) along with the matte box you are buying so that you will be able to copy slides and movie frames with your matte box. Being able to copy a single movie frame, of course, allows you to introduce a freeze frame, in which a single frame can be held still for any length of time you choose. You simply copy the particular frame in which the desired action appears while it is held in place in the matte box. The frame or slide to be copied is usually put in the rear (smaller) opening of the matte box. An opal glass or sheet of excellent diffusing plastic, such as that put out by Piolite Plastics, 210 Essex Ave., Gloucester, Mass. 01930, is put in the larger opening of the matte box. A #2 photoflood in a reflector set about two feet in front of the matte box should give you good exposure if you stop down to $f/4$ for ASA 40 tungsten-rated film. Make some film tests, however, before using up a lot of film. Once your trial exposures indicate the perfect setting for a few different densities of slides and/or frames, you ought to be able to judge most exposures quite well. Just try to stick to using the same light, at the same distance and angle, each time. An accurate, selective-type exposure meter, such as the Weston Ranger 9, which can read a small section, should be of great help in checking correct exposure. If your camera has a built-in automatic exposure meter that reads a small area of the scene and sets the aperture on the basis of the reading, the meter should be switched if possible from automatic exposure to manual and your exposure should be determined by experience and a good external selective-reading meter.

The traveling (moving) mask effect can be used to separate an important segment of a scene. For example, suppose you wish to show a vital part of a complicated machine. A square, round, or diamond-shaped mask, mounted in the front frame of the matte box can be set so that it does not show at the beginning of the sequence which shows the whole machine. As the scene moves toward the last third of the total footage, move the mask, for instance a diamond cut out of the central part of the mask, gradually from the camera lens so that, at the end of the scene, only the most vital part of the machine lies within the shaped area. This scene could be followed by another much closer picture, showing just the area that had been singled out by the mask in a normal full frame. Remember, when shooting through a mask that your exposure is based completely on the brightness of the scene you are photographing. Make no compensation for the mask.

The matte box may be used to create all manner of wipes. A wipe is a very useful device as it allows continuity to remain intact when, in fact, it has been interrupted. A wipe indicates to the audience that what has gone before is definitely finished and that something new is about to start. Thus, by simply introducing a wipe at the end of a scene as the mask covers more and more of the field of vision, you eliminate the need for the prior scene to lead smoothly into the next. You open your next scene by fading in or wiping in, so that the beginning of the new scene and new line of thought gradually covers more and more of the screen (in the case of a wipe-in) until the new scene fills the frame. The mask has been moved gradually across the screen until it is completely out of the field of view. It is best, of course, to use the front frame with the mask set as far from the camera lens as possible so that the matte box does not cut into the picture at any point, once the mask is completely removed. Many types of wipes are possible. For a diagonal wipe, just cut a mask diagonally to the matte frame. For an irregular wipe, cut a mask in an irregular saw-toothed manner on either a diagonal or vertical line. Naturally, you can use the same masks for either vertical or horizontal wipes.

Wipes can also be combined with other masks, e.g., binoculars, heart, keyhole. The matte box guides should have two grooves, so the wipe mask can be moved in front, or behind, another mask. This allows combinations of effects. Remember that wipes should be executed smoothly and quickly. They should be on the screen not more than two seconds. One second and $1\frac{1}{2}$ seconds are usually excellent wipe times.

The matte box can also be used in title-making. You will learn more about this in the chapter on titling (7). We have just scratched the surface of special effect photography via the matte box. The matte box can be used as a stand for macrocinematography. A good matte box provides a perfect perpendicular to the optical axis of the lens, which is ideal for close-ups. For shadowless pictures or for creating the illusion of things floating in air, the subject is placed directly on the glassplate (cut to fit and slid into place) in the small rear opening of the matte box; the background is set up several inches behind it. For backlighted effects, the subject is placed on a piece of opal glass or opaque diffusing plastic in the large front opening of the matte box. The light is then placed behind the opal glass or plastic. This makes an excellent setup for shooting extreme close-ups of leaves, flowers, butterflies, insects, and other miniature subjects.

There is a lot more to special effects than the matte box, and you will read more about some of them in other areas of this book. There is, however, no way of doing such a multitude of special effects so simply, professionally, and inexpensively, as with a matte box. Get one, and enjoy instant success in the accomplishment of special effects!

2

Filters, Prisms, and Lens Attachments

Many people think the only time you add a piece of glass to your camera lens is when you place a filter on your camera while shooting black-and-white film; nothing could be further from the truth. In this chapter, we shall discuss in depth, among other things, filters that can and often should be used with color film. First a word of advice, however. One of the easiest ways to waste money in photography is by buying various sets of filters and attachments to fit various size lenses. This is totally unnecessary. Determine the largest diameter of lens you use. Buy all your filters to fit this size; then simply buy step-down adapter rings so that all your filters may be used on any of your lenses. I have all my filters in Series 7 size now; this means that I can use any of them with all my lenses, motion-picture, still, and videotape. The only lenses for which I need separate filters are my zoom 85mm-300mm lens and those lenses that require such large sizes that use with any ordinary camera would be impractical. With adapter rings, however, Series 7 filters can be used on 16mm and Super 8mm movie cameras, as well as 25mm, $2\frac{1}{4}$ x $2\frac{1}{4}$, and 4 x 5 still cameras. The Series 7 can even be adapted to Ampex videotape equipment.

Close-up Lenses

One attachment that should be fully explored is the close-up lens. By attaching one of these lenses to your normal camera lens you can make extreme close-ups in situations where you cannot get close enough with the camera lens. Often these lenses are sold in sets. A set of three, for instance, might contain +1, +2, and +3 diopter lenses that can be screwed into one another for still greater magnification. A close-up lens set tremendously enlarges the scope of your photographic possibilities whether you are doing still, motion-picture, or videotape photography. Obviously close-up lenses have no use if you can achieve the same effect with a lens of proper focal length or with a bellows attachment (such as on view-type cameras). Only use the close-up attachments if you lack proper equipment for the close-up situation. Never buy equipment for which you have no use. Unnecessary items just clutter up your gadget bag.

Fig. 2-1

Fig. 2-2

Special Lens Attachments

Figure 2-1 shows four extremely useful attachments to put over a lens to achieve special effects as well as to solve a multitude of photographic problems in a most efficient and practical manner. These attachments are:

(A) *Prisma Lens* (top of picture): This lens creates multiple images and is formed in the shape of a central square area with four equal sides slanting down from it. The slanted sides are shaped like prisms. It looks like clear glass and does not alter color.

(B) *Duto Lens* (slightly to the right and resting on top of the lower right side of the Prisma Lens): This is simply a soft-focus lens, *not* a filter. It will not change either the color or black-and-white rendition of a subject. It softens and slightly diffuses *all* rays.

(C) *Pola-Screen* (just below the Prisma Lens): Composed of blackish-looking glass, this lens can be used to darken the sky in either black-and-white or color, to cut out unwanted reflections, or to help eliminate haze. It can also be used as a neutral density filter, since it has a filter factor of $4\times$. This means that putting the Pola-Screen over the lens is equivalent to closing down the lens two f/stops.

(D) *Cross Screen* (resting on top of the Duto Lens and Pola-Screen): Imbedded in the glass of this attachment is a silvery wire resembling bright mosquito screen. It creates little starlike flares on highlights — a glitter effect — very useful for night and water scenes.

The Pola-Screen is tinted a gray shade. The other three attachments are made with clear optical glass of fine lens quality. None of these are filters in that they absorb no part of the light spectrum: they are neutral in respect both to hues in color film and to rendition of gray tones in black-and-white.

The Prisma Lens, Duto Lens, Pola-Screen, and Cross Screen are all made by the Samigon Corporation. Further information about their full line of auxiliary lenses may be obtained by writing Samigon Corp., 153 W. 19th St., New York, N. Y. 10011. Other firms that are among those who should be consulted on the questions related to filters are: Eastman Kodak, Rochester, N. Y. — Eastman always has an excellent supply of information on almost anything connected with photography — Ednalite, and Tiffen. Still more sources may be found in the *Photo-Dealer Directory* (which I advise you to procure) and by consulting with your local camera shop.

It does not pay to put a poor-quality filter over your lens, because the filter in effect becomes a component of the taking lens. You should not detract from the fine optical quality of the lens by muzzling its capabilities with the imperfection of less-than-optical-quality glass in the form of poor-quality filters. I realize there will be times when, for special effects, you will shoot through ordinary glass, but I don't recommend this as regular practice.

Prisma Lens

In Fig. 2-2 is a Samigon Prisma Lens attached to a Bell & Howell Super 8mm movie camera. The little handle pointing from the right side of the

Primsa Lens to the top right corner of this picture is used to rotate the lens. When the Prisma Lens is rotated slowly, the multiple images it creates are also rotated. The camera is mounted on a special white-painted bracket that I designed to accept the *matte box*, which I use for many special effects. It locks into the black bracket mounted on the forward face of the inverted white L-bracket.

In Fig. 2-3 you can see an example of the hilarious, and effective, photographic magic and fun you can create with the Prisma Lens. The true, or central, image is formed by the central flat section of optical glass parallel to the film plane. The four additional figures are formed by the four prismatic sections that slant down from the center square of "normal" flat area and out to the sides of the rim of the Prisma Lens. I have tried ways recommended by books, using mirrors arranged in a triangle, to create similar multi-images. However, these create images only in a limited and, to me, most unsatisfactory manner. If you are going to create an effect as good and professional as this one, so loaded with excellent possibilities, please take my advice: Pay the price for the Prisma Lens and do it right! You will find that the film and time you save and the great fun you'll have will be well worth the investment.

Figure 2-4 shows single frames taken from different points along a strip of movie film exposed while the handle on the Prisma Lens was being rotated. These frames illustrate the following points:

1. The additional figures rotate around the central figure as the motion-picture film advances through the camera, or as the videotape runs through the videotape recorder.

Fig. 2-4

2. During rotation, the additional figures become more transparent or more "solid" in relation to their position to the lighting of the scene. You can, of course, control this with your lighting. For example, the strongest light source in this scene is to the right; consequently, the strongest images are created on the right side of the picture.

3. The Prisma Lens can produce many excellent still pictures in addition to its movie and videotape possibilities. By simple rotation of the Prisma Lens, you may select any one of many combinations of images.

The Prisma Lens is so easy to use that it requires little explanation. It may be used with either color or black-and-white. Also, there are Prisma Lenses available that provide more than five images. Prisms represent a whole field of practical uses and special effects. Once you use them and begin to explore their possibilities, you will find the fun and professional quality of your photography developing an entirely new aspect. If you are deeply interested, you might try to find a local optician, preferably one who has an interest in photography, and go over with him what prisms are available, what the different ones can do, and what they cost.

One warning, however: *Never* let technique take over, and *never* ignore the principles of intelligent communication and good story-telling.

In the series of pictures illustrating the use of the Prisma Lens, a *story* is told; the Prisma Lens is objectively utilized to tell that story a little more effectively and entertainingly. The bridge player has had a little too much to drink and has come up with a fantastic "hand." He is, with a feeling of sly effectiveness, bidding toward a climax of high points, not realizing that he has carefully arranged his "hand" so it may be seen by everyone at the table.

The follow-up scenes would be of his fellow players (without the Prisma Lens), then of the "looped" player looking down at his cards. As he looks down at his cards, you could show the close-up of the hand of cards again through the Prisma Lens, rotating slower and slower. Next you could remove the Prisma Lens, come from a slightly out-of-focus "blur" to a sharp image of the cards in the hand from the player's point of view (the backs of the cards facing the camera, as they would him). A sharp medium shot showing the player and his hands would be next. As he suddenly and fully realizes what he has done, he puts the cards, face-up, in the center of the table, lays his head in his hands, and begins to cry. Climax shot is close-up of the beautiful hand of cards. Naturally, you may intermingle some shots of the other players so that they contribute even more to the climax. Avoid overworking the Prisma Lens by interjecting scenes taken without the Prisma Lens, so that when the Prisma Lens scenes come on, they hit with extra impact. Do not overuse these scenes or the effect will lose its punch. Always use common sense; don't work a good thing to death!

Duto Lens

Some of the most priceless scenes (still, movie, or videotape), whether personal or professional, are often the "natural" ones, enacted in common surroundings. The series of frames in Figs. 2-5 and 2-6 is a selection of such scenes; they could be either a series of still shots or frames from movies or videotape. The story is a dual portrait of great grandma, beloved babysitter, and great grandchild. The trouble is that the needle-like sharpness of today's lenses is murder on anything but a baby's skin in close-ups.

Fig. 2-5a

Fig. 2-5b

Fig. 2-5c

Fig. 2-5d

Fig. 2-6a   Fig. 2-6b

Fig. 2-6c   Fig. 2-6d

Originally, Figs. 2-5a, b, and c made up the three scenes in Fig. 2-5, all of which were done with the camera lens alone. Figures 2-6a, b, and c were shot the same way. As you can see in the illustrations, 5c was removed and 5d was substituted for the close-up scene. In Fig. 2-6, 6c was removed and 6d substituted. Both 5d and 6d were shot with the Duto Lens over the shooting lens. This diffusing lens renders the close-up of great grandma with a little more flattery, softening wrinkles, lines, and other imperfections of age. Again, there is a technique to utilizing such a lens; you do not wish the change from crisp clarity to diffusion and softness to be too abrupt, so you should make the switch as you make a change in image size when you move in for a close-up. Do not first shoot great grandma *with* the soft-focus Duto Lens and then switch immediately to a close-up of baby *without* the Duto Lens. The technique to follow is to move in for a close-up of the older person with the Duto Lens in place and make the soft-focus scene; then move back for a medium or long shot showing both subjects in sharp focus without the Duto Lens. The exceptional clarity, so obvious in close-ups, would not seem to come on with such an abrupt jolt. The audience only remembers clearly one or two scenes back, so when you make a change in method of shooting, and therefore in technique of presentation, you should do it through shots which more smoothly allow for this type of transition. Do not make the switch back-to-back unless you are making a film utilizing abrupt changes of scene content and technique as a part of the scheme of things — for instance, in a rapid-sequence crazy-quilt type of film (babies and great grandmas are rarely featured in these). Good presentation, logical progression, continuity of thought, smoothness of technique are *not* normally abandoned in special effects. The trick technique should

40

be woven into the overall fabric of scenes so that it contributes to the pleasure and enjoyment of viewing without disrupting the weave of the presentation.

The Duto Lens has many applications; not the least among these is the soft and restful picturing of scenic outdoor locations. A many-splendored fall scene, a brook or small waterfall in the woods, a small harbor on a misty morning — the applications in which soft rendition can contribute much to a scene are without end. The Duto Lens requires no change in exposure; thus its use with other filters in any of many possible combinations will inflict no problem in respect to either exposure or color. It is completely neutral except for its power to induce a softness in imagery.

Again, don't overwork the technique or the device. It is always best for the viewer to wish he had seen more than to regret having seen too much — of either a subject *or* a technique. The trick should be a treat — not just a trick!

Pola-Screen

One of the most useful devices you can ever have is the Pola-Screen. It has a filter factor — usually about $4\times$, which means that using it requires opening up about two *f*/stops. It can darken blue sky beautifully. Professional still and motion-picture photographers are also well acquainted with its ability to cut down on reflections and haze.

This latter capacity is often used to cut down reflections when shooting through glass, such as in store windows. In Figs. 2-7a and 7b, you see a rather subtle application of the use of my Pola-Screen. I wished to copy one of my oil paintings, which has a rather shiny surface. By careful lighting, I was able to eliminate most reflections as seen in Fig. 2-7a. Many people would have stopped there and would have accepted this photograph as adequate. What is lost through slight, almost imperceptible reflection from the surface is some of the dimension, boldness of stroke in some areas, and the contrast of the overall rendition. I hope that in this reproduction you will still be able to see the difference in Fig. 2-7b. It is a fine and subtle difference, so don't expect it to be obvious; but it *is* a difference — that fine hairline between better and best. In this case, the final touch was use of the Pola-Screen.

Because the main purpose of a polarizing filter or lens is to eliminate glare and reflective haze, the Pola-Screen is especially useful when shooting polished furniture, oil paintings, and other highly reflective surfaces. It is especially good, too, in shooting long-distance scenes in which there are a multitude of reflections and glares, ranging from those created by shiny surfaces such as water, sand, and snow to those made by tiny droplets of moisture in the air. What appears as the most insignificant vapor close up can become quite a haze and glare-producer through miles of distance.

Here, then, is a breakdown of the uses of the Pola-Screen:

1. *Dark-blue effects in color photography.* Pola-Screens offer the best means of sky-brightness control in color photography.

2. *Photographing through water or glass.* When the camera axis (line of sight through the lens) is about 35 degrees to the reflecting surface of the

41

Fig. 2-7a

subject, the Pola-Screen can cut through the reflections to show detail beyond them.

3. *Reduction of oblique reflection to get better texture rendition.* Reflections of lights or of light backgrounds can be cut down so that more texture is shown in nonmetallic surfaces when the angle of reflection is about 35 degrees to the surface. When reflections are coming from a metal surface, Pola-Screens are needed on lights, as well as on the lens, in order to cut down the reflections.

NOTE: Since the camera axis must point at a right angle to direct sunlight rays for the darkest sky effects, light will hit the subject from the side or, at noon, from overhead. This affects exposure. Also, when you are shooting through water or glass, the light reflected from the water or glass surface (and thus prevented from going through the water or glass and hitting the subject) must be taken into account. Both cases require an increase in exposure.

Normally, at least half the light reflected from the subject is absorbed by a Pola-Screen, so the exposure, especially for close subjects, should be increased by 1½ to 2 stops (a factor of 3 to 4) anyway. Thus two increases must be made. For example, to get the dark-sky effect, the scene has to be side- or top-lighted, requiring ½ to 1 stop more exposure than in a scene in which light is reflected directly from the subject into the lens. In addition, *another* 1½- to

42

Fig. 2-7b

2½-stop increase (representing a factor of from 3 to 5) should be used for the polarizing factor.

Because removal of haze by means of a Pola-Screen in landscapes in clear weather darkens the shadows as well, an exposure factor of 4 should be employed when the Pola-Screen is used to eliminate haze.

It should further be noted that the Pola-Screen can also build up the color in green foliage while darkening the blue sky of a scene.

To see for yourself how a Pola-Screen works, hold a polarizing filter up to the blue sky and rotate the filter. As the filter is turned, the sky will get darker. Then, as you turn further, the sky will once again become lighter. This experiment points up the tremendous advantage of viewing the scene through the taking lens: as you turn the Pola-Screen, you can see exactly the effect it will have on the scene or subject.

The key thing to remember about using a Pola-Screen outdoors is that the degree of polarized light from a specific part of the sky will vary with the location of that area in relation to the sun. *Maximum polarization* will occur at an angle of 90 degrees to the sun. Panning should *not* be done when the Pola-Screen is used. For when you turn the camera you vary the angle of lens-to-scene—to—sun. As you change this angle, you also change the degree of

Fig. 2-8a

Fig. 2-8b

polarization of the light, resulting in at least a variance in darkening of the sky.

Also bear in mind that other filters may be used in combination with a Pola-Screen to control color of foreground areas. You must remember to calculate the total filter factor (the factor with the Pola-Screen plus the factor of any other filter) and estimate your exposure accordingly. A behind-the-lens meter in your camera, with filter or filters in place, provides a good check on your external meter estimates.

44

Fig. 2-9c

Fig. 2-9a

Fig. 2-9b

Cross Screen

We have covered the first three of these lenses. Now let's talk about the fourth, the Cross Screen.

Figure 2-8a is just a straight shot, at night, of a section of the New York skyline. Figure 2-8b is another shot of approximately the same section of skyline from the same camera position with the same exposure, but with the Cross Screen over the camera lens. Concentrations of light are turned into blazes of illumination; other bright but more singular spots of light develop starlike sparkling crosses of light. Cross Screen effects can be altered by rotating it in the filter holder. Again, through-the-lens viewing is of prime importance. You can do best when you can see what you are doing. For motion pictures, you could single-frame, rotating the Cross Screen a little at a time so that the blaze and the sparkling would increase and diminish as successive single frames

45

were shot. In motion pictures and videotape, leave the Cross Screen set in place if no movement of the sparkling is desired. If you do wish an in-and-out sparkling and blazing but you cannot single-frame — or if there is movement in your scene — you will have to rig a filter-holder with a small handle (like the one on the Pola-Screen) so that you can slowly and carefully turn the Cross Screen while the camera is running.

In cases in which there is a great concentration of light, such as in the marquee for *The Incident* in Times Square, a straight shot should be made first (as in Fig. 2-9a). If you are going to use the Cross Screen at all, you have to use it before you get too close to the brilliant area (as in Fig. 2-9b). If you go in closer, the high concentration of light will cause quite a confusion of diffusion (if you'll excuse the expression). There is so much bright light so closely packed in one area that the Cross Screen will cause thousands of tiny light crosses to be superimposed one on top of the other just a little out of register with each other. The result may be seen in Fig. 2-9c; the lettering on the sign is actually diffused by the mix-up of light rays. Except when used deliberately for special effect, this extreme diffusion would be out of context.

Figures 2-10a and 2-10b show, respectively, a clear-cut rendition of a brightly lighted area (without Cross Screen) and the maximum treatment that would normally be acceptable with the Cross Screen lens. Figure 2-10b also shows the closest tolerable camera-to-subject distance with the Cross Screen at maximum efficiency. If you were to move in for a closer shot of either the Canadian Club or the Desert Inn signs, for example, you should remove the Cross Screen and shoot the scene straight. In fact, when you move in for any extreme close-ups of this kind, you might do well to use a Pola-Screen (without a Cross Screen).

In still pictures, you have to decide how you would use a Cross Screen effect in either a single scene or a series of single scenes. Although continuity in a series of still pictures does not have to flow as strictly from one scene to the next as in motion pictures, your picture story will flow better if you introduce the Cross Screen effect as naturally as possible. If, for example, you were showing water scenes, you could move the camera from a position from which the glare was at a minimum to a position from which the water looked glaring and sparkling even to the naked eye (that is, without a Cross Screen). This would provide you with a natural transition from scenes without to scenes with the Cross Screen. Such use of the Cross Screen would be very effective with motion pictures and videotape as well. The effect is not "special" in that it is unnatural; you would simply be accentuating natural light behavior under a particular condition. Again, I'd suggest slow rotation of the Cross Screen while the motion-picture camera is running. Unless you wish to create a rather turbulent action of water, however, you would not single-frame such a scene. Water in anything but the stillest lake is constantly moving, and by single-framing you might introduce unnatural gaps in the sequence of natural water action.

Again I suggest that you be alert to other possibilities too numerous to mention. In glary water scenes, you might try a combination of Pola-Screen and Cross Screen. Such a combination under the right lighting conditions might eliminate some of the unimportant conflicting highlights and glare and accentuate the important highlights. Only on-the-spot testing or through-the-lens viewing or both will give correct evaluation of just what to use.

Fig. 2-10a

Fig. 2-10b

The Cross Screen should not be limited only to the obvious case of accentuating many highlights. In shooting a close-up of a beautiful red rose with just one large dew-drop, using flat lighting and rotating the Cross Screen can produce just the right diamond-like sparkle to burst forth from the dew-drop in a subtle but definite manner. In stills you would set the Cross Screen at the exact point of best dramatic emphasis; in any kind of motion-picture photography, you could single-frame the close-up, rotating the Cross Screen between frames. You will actually be able to make that dew-drop scintillate! Be very careful not to jar the camera during single-framing.

Filter Factors and Filter Colors

We have been talking a lot about filter factors. What are they, and why do we need them? A filter absorbs part of the light that would ordinarily expose the film. When you are dealing with light, you should keep in mind that color in the form of light is different from paint or pigment color. Mixing red and green light in proper proportion produces pure yellow; mixing red and green pigment yields a dirty brown color. The color-sensitive sections of the retina of the human eye have elements most directly responsive to three areas of the light spectrum: blue-violet, green, and red-orange. Human vision is thus a three-color process responding to three primary colors (blue-violet, green, and red-orange). It is therefore helpful to think of filters in terms of color arithmetic, that is, as the addition or subtraction of the three primary colors, or proportions of them, to or from other primary colors.

A filter is the color it appears to be because it filters out colors different from its own. If you hold a green filter between the sun and a piece of white paper, the shadow it casts will be green; the other colors have been absorbed by the filter. Since all light has some exposure effect on film sensitive to it, the light which is absorbed by the filter can no longer take part in exposing the film. This loss of exposure power must be compensated for by longer exposure time. The filter manufacturer calculates the filter factor by ascertaining the loss of exposure power that a particular filter imposes in respect to the type of film involved. Different films can be more, or less, sensitive to different colors, whether the film is color or black-and-white. It depends upon the type of emulsion and its sensitivity to areas of the light spectrum. The filter manufacturer takes this into account when establishing the filter factor for each filter.

In black-and-white photography, panchromatic film is sensitive to light almost in the same manner in which the human eye is sensitive to light. Panchromatic film "sees" almost the same spectrum as the human eye and in the same degree, with just a little more sensitivity to blue and ultraviolet. A filter used with panchromatic film will cause objects of its own color to appear as white or very light gray in the positive print. Thus, if you put a green mark on a white piece of paper and photograph it through a filter of the same shade of green, the green mark will be filtered out and the paper will appear *totally white*. The mark will have vanished. The green filter passes green light only; thus, if dark enough green light only were to expose the film, a green mark would be completely "lost" in the overall light exposing the film.

In color photography, the green filter would build up exposure in all green

48

Plate 1. A "warm" rendition of color is shown in this arrangement of a plaster bust and color wheel, placed in direct sunlight.

Plate 2. A "cool" rendition of color is illustrated by moving the group in Plate 1 into open shade.

Plates 3-10. Demonstration of filter effects. Plate 3 (above). No filter. Plate 4 (below). Kodak CC-20C filter, light blue. Plate 5 (opposite, top). Tiffen 80B filter, dark blue. Plate 6 (opposite, middle). Light yellow-orange 11 tungsten-to-daylight conversion filter. Plate 7 (opposite, bottom). Ultraviolet filter. Plate 8 (page 4, top). Orange filter. Plate 9 (page 4, middle). Underexposure with orange filter. Plate 10 (page 4, bottom). Kodak X1 filter, dark green.

Plate 5

Plate 6

Plate 7

Plate 8

Plate 9

Plate 10

areas, darkening them. In other colored areas in the scene, the green light would mix with the different colors, changing their color rendition.

Putting all this knowledge to practical application, we can reap many benefits, including the more intelligent selection of a kit of basic filters. More about this selection in just a moment. First, however, I want you to notice one of the most important qualities of everyday light; the "warmth" and "coolness," the yellowish or bluish cast (respectively) of light that usually occurs in ordinary outdoor situations. This difference can best be illustrated by Plates 1 and 2. Shown in each of these illustrations are a pure white plaster bust placed on an artist's white canvas and an artist's color chart (black center, white background), all set on an ordinary blacktop driveway. Fieldstone wall and green grass are in the background.

Plate 1 shows normal morning light, not too bright or harsh, with some thin clouds in the sky. Notice the medium "warm" rendition of color, actually quite true in every respect. In order not to wash out the white of the bust and chart and the gray of the stones, the green grass was slightly underexposed. It was necessary, in this case, to give every major consideration to proper exposure of the color chart.

Plate 2 was taken on the same day, not more than a few minutes after the first exposure. The bust and chart have been moved along the same wall to a point at which they are in open shade. There was clear sky overhead and some sun even filtered through the leaves of a willow tree as you can see from the splotches of warmer, more yellow light. Even so, look at the buildup of blue light in the major portion of the overall scene. Note the change this makes in colors on the chart in the areas where no yellow light from the sun has penetrated. In the shaded areas, most of the light is reflected into the scene from blue sky area, so it will normally have a very high blue content.

In black-and-white photography, I almost never shoot an outdoor scene without a medium yellow filter (K2 or equivalent) over the lens. In still black-and-white shots, especially when fairly close scenes of people are involved, I often use a small flashbulb, to lighten the shadow areas, in addition to the medium yellow filter.

In shooting still color pictures, blue flashbulbs can be used for subjects lighted directly by the sun, as these bulbs are color-corrected. Even the plain bulbs, which compensate even more for excessive blue, can be used in shady locations. Color-correction filters are often used by professional photographers not only to balance certain lighting situations, but also to compensate generally for other buildups of incorrect hues. For example, if a subject is wearing a bright red shirt, the red hue will reflect into his face, causing it to look unnaturally red. This can be adjusted by using a filter that will compensate for the excessive red.

There is no such thing as being able to tell you exactly what to do under every set of circumstances. There are just too many variances. I can, however, direct you to various areas of experimentation. I strongly suggest that you get a blackboard slate; for each test shot, list on the blackboard your meter reading, your exposure, and filter used. Photograph the blackboard in the scene so when your film is developed you may read exactly what you did in the test. In this way you will educate yourself far better than anyone who tries to give you all the answers. You learn best by doing.

Filters in Black-and-White Photography

Yellow filters are most common. The K2 yellow filter (or equivalent) is probably the most used of these. It darkens blue sky and water. For more contrast and a greater darkening of sky, water, etc., filters used range from light orange to deep red. Contrast filters are sometimes used to get a night effect in daylight. Simulated night effects can be created better by using a red filter and underexposing. However, if there are flesh tones in the scene, a red filter may wash out skin, as there is a lot of red pigmentation in flesh areas. In this event you might try using a combination of filters. For example, in the Kodak filters, you could combine a No. 23A with a No. 56 filter. By then underexposing, you would obtain more natural flesh tones in the simulated night shots.

Since definite factors are not usually given for obtaining night effects in daylight, and since the increase of exposure will vary with the degree of "night" you wish to simulate, you can understand why filter-makers stay away from being too specific in regard to the use of their product for special effects. As a rough guide and a basis for your experimentation, however, you may utilize the following rule of thumb:

FILTER	EXPOSURE INCREASE
23A or equivalent	3 times
25 or equivalent	5 times
29 or 72B or equivalent	12 times
23A used in combination with 56	6 times

NOTE: The above is for regular black-and-white panchromatic film.

Filters in Color Photography

The most explicit impression that can be given of what happens when a colored filter is used over the lens is to show you eight pictures of the same scene shot as nearly as possible under the same conditions, but with different filters.

Plate 3: Taken without any filter, normal exposure for the scene.

Plate 4: Slightly underexposed with light blue filter (Kodak color-compensating CC-20C) over lens.

Plate 5: Underexposed with dark blue filter (Tiffen 80B) over lens.

Plate 6: Light yellow-orange 11 tungsten-to-daylight conversion filter over lens.

Plate 7: Underexposed with ultraviolet filter comparable to Kodak CC-13 over lens.

Plate 8: Light exposure, slightly overexposed with orange filter over lens (about 25 in the red series).

Plate 9: Dark exposure, underexposure with the same orange filter over lens. Plates 8 and 9 were included to illustrate the color control possible with the same filter by changing exposure alone. Note the color buildup in the under-exposed scene in Plate 9.

Plate 10: Made with a fairly dark green Kodak filter X1 over lens; slightly underexposed.

This comparison should illustrate the cold, night effect an excess of blue brings to a scene, the sunset warmth of orange, and the springtime effect of green. All shots were made on Kodachrome Daylight transparency film, which is corrected for normal daylight without any filter. For general use, I suggest Kodachrome II, Type A tungsten film and using a tungsten-to-daylight conversion filter over the lens for all shooting. Super 8mm movie cameras normally have this conversion filter built into the camera, and it is left in position when shooting outdoors. When you shoot indoors with Super 8mm, the filter is removed from the lens.

Tungsten film, when shot outdoors or under color-corrected lights without the tungsten-to-daylight filter in place, will have a bluish cast because normal indoor lights are quite red in color, not white like full-spectrum outdoor light. Thus, using tungsten color film such as Kodachrome II, Type A, you can get a simulated night effect in daylight by removing the tungsten-to-daylight filter from the lens, shooting the daylight scene from an angle so that you have a contrasty lighting, and underexposing. Reduce your exposure ½ to 2 stops. If additional darkening of the sky is desired you may use a Pola-Screen over the lens. If a night effect is desired, a blue filter can be used following the above instructions, with or without the Pola-Screen. How dark a blue would be determined by how dark you wish the night effect to be. Conduct your own tests to find the degrees of these effects that are best suited to your purposes.

Facts in themselves are not really practical knowledge; it is only when you are able to apply the facts to various situations that you can be supposed to have practical knowledge. For example, in black-and-white photography you now know that a filter will lighten its own color. Suppose you had a piece of mahogany wood: how could you make its grain stand out? The main area of the wood is essentially red and the grain is blackish. Thus a red filter would lighten the general wood areas between the blackish grain, and the contrast between grain and wood would be increased. This would make the grain show up more. If you wished to render the wood even more carefully you might try using, in combination with the red filter, a Pola-Screen to kill surface reflection.

In the case of color, if you wished to emphasize the red of the mahogany wood, you would want to redden the tone of the wood slightly without making the black of the grain muddy. A slight orange filter such as a tungsten-to-daylight conversion type would pick up the red without darkening the black of the wood grain. If you already are using Type A tungsten film and shooting the mahogany wood indoors under normal indoor lighting, the redness of the regular light plus the warmth of the conversion filter might be sufficient. Again, it would be informative to see what effect the Pola-Screen would have in conjunction with the tungsten-to-daylight filter.

For you to gauge which color filters to use under differing circumstances, I suggest you get a color chart such as the one shown in Plates 1 and 2. This is a Hilar Color Chart, made in San Francisco, Calif. They can usually be bought at any well-stocked art supply store. Buy a large one. Just remember one thing: The Hilar chart calls the three primary colors yellow (#1 on the chart shown), magenta (#6), and cyan (#10). Do not be confused by this. These are primaries for filters. Light primaries are: blue (approximately between #9 and #8 on the Hilar chart); green (about #13 on chart); and red (about #4 on chart).

In talking about chart numbers I refer to the white numbers on the black central section of the chart. The number lies in the pointed area of black on its color: #1 is at 12 o'clock, #9 at 6 o'clock, and #10 at about 7 o'clock.

I have suggested you get a large version of this chart so that you may see the effect of any filter more easily when you view the chart through a filter. If you do this you will discover that a reddish-orange filter — such as a 25, which is almost scarlet by the Hilar chart evaluation — will lighten its own color or anything having yellow or red in it, tinting them slightly red. This same filter will darken anything having blue or green in it, and redden everything from violet through red. A green filter will lighten the blues and greens and darken violets and reds, and so on. Try to train your eye to see how any color, put over your lens, will affect every color in a scene. The next step, of course, is actually to view the scene through the colored filter and see exactly what effect that filter will have on the scene. The chart only helps you to see more clearly what might be too subtle for you to observe in the actual scene until you get accustomed to looking through colored filters directly at scenes to be photographed.

Normally, leaving the tungsten-to-daylight conversion filter in place over film like Kodachrome II, Type A and using a Pola-Screen on sky, water, etc. will give you all the correction you'll need. However, if you wish to make a sunset even more spectacular, add more red by using another light orange or very light red filter.

A good working knowledge of fundamental "tricks of the trade" of filters will stand you in good stead. Suppose you had to shoot a scene in a well-lit classroom near windows, with sunlight streaming in. Both incandescent (reddish) and fluorescent (bluish) bulbs supply additional illumination. This is a real lighting problem in terms of color rendition. Remember that window glass is not colorless but somewhat greenish in cast. The glass tends to absorb ultraviolet rays, killing part of the blue end of the spectrum. Since the red and yellow end of the light spectrum is not affected by the rays' passing through the glass, and since there is some reddish light being added to the fluorescent bulbs by the ordinary indoor lights inside the room, we must give the violet end of the spectrum a little boost. Try a magenta filter. A shade of magenta will usually correct this problem. This filter tends to add more violet than scarlet or yellow, usually just enough to effect fine correction.

As a suggestion for a basic filter kit, beyond those filters we have already mentioned, I list the following, as they will serve a multitude of purposes, often in both black-and-white and color photography:

Type*	Filter Color	Filter Factor	Effect and/or Purpose†
80B	Deep blue	3	Night effects in color. In black-and-white, lightens blue.
82A	Light blue	1.5	Light night effects in color. Cuts down excessive red-yellow tint in twilight. In black-and-white, lightens blue.
85B	Deep amber	2	Converts indoor film to outdoor. Also acts as haze filter.
K2	Medium yellow	2	Most common corrective filter for black-and-white panchromatic films (darkens blue), but also can be used to cut excessive blue in scenes.
25	Red	6	With pan black-and-white films, creates dramatic sky, simulated moonlight with slight underexposure; excellent copying filter for blueprints. If used with infrared film, extreme sky contrast, turns foliage white, cuts through haze and mist. Used in scientific photography. In color, for sunset effects and any time when emphatic reddening desired.
X1	Light green	2	With pan films, good outdoor filter for pleasing flesh tones in portraits against sky. Also good for black-and-white rendition of landscapes, flowers, and blossoms with natural sky appearance. In color for greenish spring effect, making green greener.

---

*Different manufacturers sometimes use other designations for type of filter. Your dealer will know what is equivalent.

†I have just glossed over effects and purposes. You may check into these more thoroughly by getting some filter charts from various filter-makers and seeing which filters they make for certain purposes. The idea is to have a deep blue, light blue, deep amber, medium yellow, reddish-orange, and light green. This should enable you to handle most basic variations and get an idea of effects obtainable in both black-and-white and color. Again, the best thing you can do is make actual tests with various filters on the same subjects under the same light conditions.

3

Mirrors:
Their Magic, Fun,
and Utility

Mirror, mirror, on the wall, what wondrous, magical ways you have! Our daily lives are constantly affected by mirrors, from the car's rear-view mirror to the one on the lavatory medicine cabinet. We rely so much on them, so automatically, that it rarely occurs to us that we don't really know how we look. Except when we appear in movies, still pictures, videotape, and so on, we literally never see ourselves as others see us. Many a portrait photographer is driven to despair by the oft-repeated comment, "Why, *that* doesn't look like *me!*" The statement would be true if put, "That isn't the way I normally see myself!" For usually the only time we study our appearance carefully is in a mirror, and in a mirror we are *reversed*: we judge our appearance mainly by a *reflected* image! Look in a mirror. Grasp your right ear with your right hand. You'll find you're grasping the ear that is on *your* right as you look at the reflected image in the mirror. Since that image is looking *directly back at you*, face to face, it is the *left* hand of the image holding the *left* ear of the image. Thus, with this tool, the mirror, used down through the centuries for self-study and self-appraisal, we can only see ourselves in left-to-right reversal. Because our bodies are slightly asymmetrical, mirror reversal gives us quite a different appearance.

An entire book on the subject of mirrors could not completely explore the endless avenues of creativity available with them. The idea here is to discuss a few areas of this fascinating world and to realize that what at first seems almost pure magic is based on some fundamental laws of light and rules of mathematics. My purpose simply is to stimulate your thinking so that you can adapt the mirror to your personal needs, desires, and equipment.

Creating Space

First, let's deal with one of the most prevalent problems any cameraman has: running out of space when trying to back up far enough to get most of the

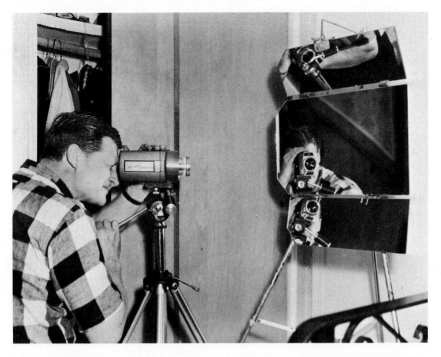

Fig. 3-2

Fig. 3-1

Fig. 3-3

people in a crowded room into the scene, or when working in close quarters, such as the stateroom of a ship. Figure 3-1 was shot off a mirror. The cameraman actually shot the scene from *outside* the room. The mirror was placed in a spot and at an angle from which a camera could not have been operated. By shooting the scene reflected from the mirror, the cameraman greatly increased his photographic "space." He made the image of the room turn a corner to enter his camera lens!

Figure 3-2 shows a simple but very flexible setup for "mirror shooting." It consists of a lightweight, inexpensive artist's easel and a tri-sectional vanity mirror. The center section is the only part being used to make this scene; the reflections in the flaps are not. The main mirror, turned sideways, has its lower side resting on the adjustable picture-holders attached to each forward leg of the easel. These are L-shaped rods, which are normally turned with the base of the L forward and up to prevent the canvas from sliding while the artist paints. For our use, the holders have been turned so they are down over the bottom mirror flap to prevent their sticking up into the main mirror and, consequently, into the scene. The easel tilt-guide, which is normally fastened to the top of a painting, is securely tightened onto what is now the top edge of the mirror flap at top right of Fig. 3-2. Once the tri-sectional vanity mirror is thus secured, it is a simple matter to tilt, turn, and adjust the middle mirror so that it will reflect the desired scene into the camera lens.

If you are going to do much "mirror shooting," strive toward owning equipment that will simplify matters for you. An artist's easel, such as the one shown, should be lightweight, easily adjustable in height, and have a convenient mirror-holder and tilter. Your movie camera, like the Bell & Howell shown, should have some means of checking focus through the lens. It should also have through-the-lens scene viewing so that you have no parallax problem. Since you will often work at distances shorter than six feet from the reflecting mirror, if you were to view the scene through a lens separate from the shooting lens, you obviously would not see through the viewfinder exactly what the film will expose through the taking lens. The difference in fields of view caused by lenses set apart from each other in this way is called "parallax," and you want a camera that will not create it. It is also a tremendous advantage to have a zoom lens, such as the camera shown here. A zoom lens enables you to change the area of the mirror that you will actually shoot, quickly and easily, without touching either the mirror or your camera tripod. If you see something showing at the edge of the scene that you wish to eliminate, you can "zoom" in just far enough to eliminate anything undesireable from the field of view of the camera.

A fully adjustable tripod, like the Quick-Set shown, is also an advantage, as fine adjustments can be made to straighten or tilt the camera left or right as well as up and down. In addition, the camera may be cranked slowly upward or downward — all without moving the tripod legs. This demonstrates the old truth: tools don't create skill but skill is magnified, simplified, and most effectively applied with fine equipment. If you really enjoy a hobby or develop a craft such as photography, do it right. If you don't, you only stunt your growth, destroy much of your enjoyment, and impair the possibilities of achievement.

Viewing Fig. 3-2, remember that you are not looking into the mirror from the cameraman's angle. If you moved around to look through the viewfinder, you'd find the camera is enough left of center (to the side of the main mirror) so that the images of the camera and of the cameraman are not reflected onto the film of the movie camera. The motion-picture cameraman has zoomed in close enough to the mirror so that all the camera sees is the scene shown in Fig. 3-3. The purpose of this scene was to check out the general impression made by one of the author's oil paintings seen hanging over the dining room buffet as one enters the foyer. In Fig. 3-3, the mirror was placed in the foyer, by the front door, in the position of someone entering. Then the scene as shown reflected into the mirror (Fig. 3-3) was shot. Often, the viewer will not notice that the scene is reversed unless letters or numbers are shown. Groups of people at a

56

Fig. 3-4

Fig. 3-5

Fig. 3-6

party often pose no problem because reversal of the scene will still show who was there and what was going on. Usually, the actual arrangement of the people and furniture is of secondary importance.

A reversed image may be a problem if you are doing an instructional film, a series of slides, or a technical videotape, in which accuracy of every detail might be required. Suppose, for example, you were attempting to show exactly how the working parts of a piano action looked from the direction of the piano strings. It would be impossible to get a camera far enough away from the hammers, and still keep it between the strings and the felt hammers of the action (the moving parts connected to the felt hammers) in order to take such a shot. In Fig. 3-4, you see how this problem was solved. The lid of the piano was raised far enough to be out of the way. A rectangular piece of unframed mirror was placed behind the hammers, which strike the strings when the piano is played.

57

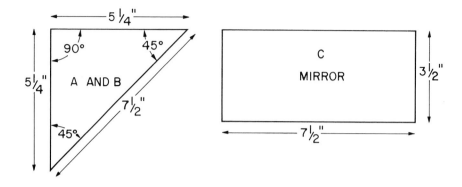

Fig. 3-7

This mirror was placed at such an angle that the image of the hammers and that section of the action are reflected straight up between the rear, rounded ends of the piano hammers and the piano strings opposite them. At this point, there is a reversed image being reflected upward, out of the piano. By placing the larger, white-framed mirror atop the piano and slanting this mirror approximately parallel to the first mirror below it (down inside the piano), we are able to reverse the image reflected to the camera back to a true image. (This area is pointed out by the black arrow and encircled in Fig. 3-4.)

You can easily see how the foregoing use of *two* mirrors would solve many problems in photographing automotive parts, pianos, electronic equipment, and any other complicated machinery. You can put mirrors in all kinds of places where cameras won't even fit — much less operate. With any even number of mirrors (two, four, six, and so on), the image will be a *true* image when it enters the lens of the camera; with any odd number of mirrors (one, three, five, and so on), the image as it is recorded by the camera will be reversed.

Although it is not an absolutely true comparison, I call the mirror the "poor man's wide-angle lens." Mirrors can give you many of the advantages of a wide-angle lens, often with considerably less distortion and vastly more opportunity to improvise on location and to solve other problems peculiar to a particular setting, circumstance, and subject matter.

Chances are that you will wish to make some equipment incorporating mirrors. I suggest you make a "mock-up," or model, first, of cardboard, using masking tape to hold the parts together temporarily, so that you can try different sizes of mirrors, openings, and angles for the mirrors. When you find exactly the construction that works best for your equipment and your uses, then duplicate the mock-up with a permanent metal or wood construction.

Figure 3-5 shows an excellent basic mirror mock-up from its open side. Figure 3-6 shows the same mock-up from the other side. With a piece of equipment like this, it is wise to make it so that it can be revolved. Then you can shoot up, or down, or sideways. The setup is in place in a Bolex matte box.

Figure 3-7 shows the plans for our simple but useful mirror device. It is of a size that can be used with most 8mm, 16mm, and 35mm motion-picture and still cameras as well as with most videotape equipment fitted with standard size lenses. If you wish to use it with larger equipment, just increase all the dimensions in necessary proportion to the size of lens involved. To make this mock-up in cardboard, cut *two* right (90-degree) triangles, "A" and "B." Since they are identical, only one drawing is shown, having 5¼-inch-long legs on the 90-degree angle and a 7½-inch-long base as shown. Use a mirror 7½ inches long by 3½ inches wide along the 7½-inch side. This is the device shown in Figs. 3-5 and 3-6. Not shown in the drawing is the "frame" used on one of the 5¼-inch sides through which the camera lens may peer. The other 5¼-inch side is left open. When you are satisfied that the mock-up suits your needs, then make it up of rigid materials and incorporate a plate, or other arrangement, for fastening it to either camera or tripod so it will be held firmly in place in front of the camera lens. The device that I constructed for the Bolex matte box is excellent. You can see this device by looking at Figs. 3-5 and 3-6 again; it is the white-painted, L-shaped metal plate that runs between the camera and the tripod head plate past the camera. Point the L-shaped base leg downward, so that the matte-box may be attached in front of the camera. This single mirror device will, of course, produce a reversed image on the film.

If you look at Fig. 3-8, you will see how you can create a device that will yield a true image and still allow you to shoot either side, up, down, and so on. Actually, it is a crude periscope. You'll have to experiment with various sizes of mirrors and different dimensions for your equipment, but the general layout for the device shown here can always be used. There is a window in front of the camera. This window is a cut-out with no glass in it. Just beyond this window is a mirror, tilted at angle "B," which is a 45-degree angle. This mirror is set parallel to another mirror directly above it. The top mirror has a window in the opposite side of the hollow box. When the image "E" is reflected off the top

Fig. 3-8

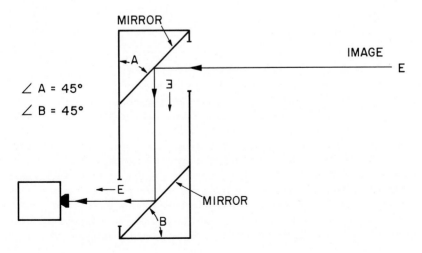

∠ A = 45°

∠ B = 45°

59

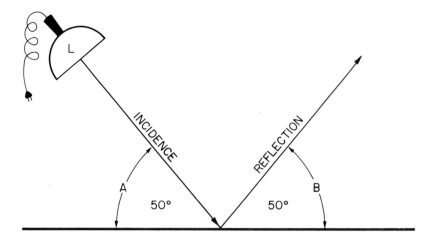

Fig. 3-9

Fig. 3-10

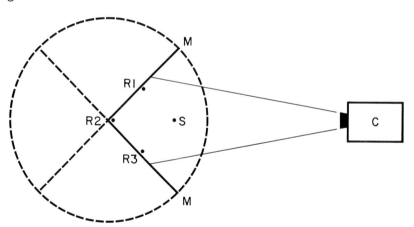

mirror, it is reversed and is shown on the blackboard as a backwards "E". This image travels directly down to the mirror below where it is reversed back to normal ("E"). This righted image is reflected into the camera. Incidentally, if you go to the trouble to make such a device, make it long enough so that it can act as a periscope to enable your camera to "see" over the heads of a crowd at a parade, the fences, and over similar obstacles. Thus, you can use it to take unobstructed pictures in such instances. Again, I advise some careful research via the cardboard mock-up before making your final equipment. You may want to experiment with a smaller mirror at the camera and a larger mirror at the opposite end of the "periscope." You may even wish to try irregular mirror shapes. Experimentation is both informative and rewarding.

60

Mirrors as Reflective Surfaces

At this juncture, I'd like to touch upon some properties of mirrors themselves. Most of the time, any good, clear mirror will do the job for you. However, if you are shooting a brightly illuminated subject in any direction except directly head-on, your camera may record a double image, one from the silver on the back of the glass (which turns the piece of glass into a mirror) and the other from the front surface of the glass itself. The image reflecting from the silver is the one you want; the other, dimmer, ghost image from the front of the glass is unwanted. The thicker the glass, the greater the danger of the ghost image intruding, for the front surface and the silver backing are further apart when the glass is thicker. With a less expensive mirror, with thinner glass, you run less risk of double-image than with a plate-glass mirror. The thinner mirrors are also lighter in weight, an advantage in location work. With a metal mirror you do not have this problem at all. A two-way mirror also eliminates this problem, as the forward face of such a mirror *is* a reflective surface. If you are going into mirror-shooting extensively, I suggest you experiment with these different types of mirrors in due course. Right now, the inexpensive, thinner glass mirror will probably not pose any serious problems and will serve well to introduce you to this intriguing field of photography.

At this point, also, we need a little blackboard "skull-practice" in *why* mirrors work. In Fig. 3-9 we see an essential law of light behavior simply illustrated. Beams of light travel in a straight line — until they hit another surface. If the surface is polished and perfectly flat (as a mirror is), then the light coming from light source L strikes the flat surface at an angle of 50 degrees (angle A). This is the *angle of incidence*. The light is then reflected off the flat surface at the same angle but in the opposite direction. This angle B is the *angle of reflection*, also 50 degrees. The law of light involved is: *The angle of reflection equals the angle of incidence but is opposite in direction.*

Look at Fig. 3-10, and consider that, whatever angle your mirrors form, that angle is part of a 360-degree circle. Thus, if you wanted to record a total of four identical images, which would mean you would show the actual image and three reflected ones for a total of four, you would divide a complete circle by four. A circle, 360 degrees, divided by 4 gives you 90 degrees. Place the two mirrors adjacent to each other so they form a 90-degree angle. Set them up as shown in Fig. 3-10, with the camera C and the subject S placed in the illustrated relationship to the mirrors. The camera will shoot the original subject plus three reflected images R1, R2, and R3, for a total of four images. For a total of five images, you would use an angle of 72 degrees, and so on.

Focusing

If you do not have a camera with through-the-lens focusing, I must warn you to be careful of your estimation of distance when you set your focusing scale. Figure 3-11 illustrates how considerable confusion can take place. Let's assume you have set up two mirrors parallel to each other, with the front mirror

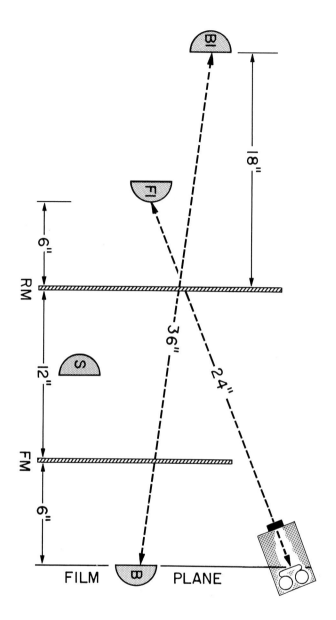

Fig. 3-11

FM six inches in front of the camera C, with the reflective side facing away from the camera and toward the rear mirror RM. The rear mirror is set 12 inches from the front mirror with its reflective side facing the front mirror and the camera. The subject S is centered between the two mirrors, six inches from each. The film plane of the camera is 18 inches from the reflective surface and 24 inches from the image "F1" (the image that is the first reflection and shows the *front* of the subject). The film plane is what counts, not the lens, because it is the film that actually receives the final image. The question is:

62

At what distance do you set your focusing scale? If you answered 24 inches you are right. It simplifies matters if you understand that, as far as the camera eye is concerned, the image reflected in the mirror is *real*, located in real space. Since the actual subject is 6 inches in front of the surface of the mirror, its reflected image is located 6 inches behind the mirror RM. The distance 24 inches is arrived at by adding the distance from F1 to RM (6 inches) and that from RM to the film plane (18 inches).

In order to determine the focusing distance to "B1," the second reflected image (which is the back of the actual subject), add the distance its image is behind the surface of FM (6 inches), the distance from FM to RM (12 inches), and the distance from RM to the film plane (18 inches). The total is 36 inches. The reasoning behind this formula is that B1 *looks* to the camera as if it is 18 inches behind the surface of RM. The image in RM is a reflection of the real distance between RM and FM plus the mirror space in which B1 resides behind the surface of FM. The image B1 reflected in RM is therefore a total of 36 inches away from the film plane. With through-the-lens focusing, you simply focus on the reflection you want in focus and do not go through any of these calculations.

Unwanted Reflections

Another problem you are going to encounter continually when shooting off mirrors is that of keeping unwanted reflections — of lights, camera, and camera-man — out of your scene. When using just one mirror, shooting at the mirror from an angle will normally eliminate unwanted images. When using more than one mirror — two for instance — I find that putting the mirrors off-center to each other (either from side-to-side or up-and-down, horizontally or vertically) is most effective.

Figure 3-12 shows an arrangement with the mirrors off-center horizontally. It also shows an excellent way of handling the lighting of the subject. Remember, you are primarily concerned with the lighting of the subject as the lighting will appear to the section of mirror actually being photographed *not* in relation to the camera. In this diagram the light source L is placed above, to the side, and just slightly in front of the subject S, which faces the rear mirror RM. However, care has been taken to keep the light and direct rays from it from striking the camera C. Since the back of the subject is also going to be shown both in reflected images and directly into camera from the actual image, care has been taken so that the light will "spill" around the subject over almost half its back; and, even more helpfully, the light will shine directly onto the lower portion of the mirror and reflect quite a bit of illumination onto the back of the subject. You don't want to shine the light too high up on the surface of the front mirror, as you may create a glare or "haze" of brilliancy. In cases like this, watch the angle of the light.

The front mirror in Fig. 3-12 is slightly lower than the top of the rear mirror; the camera is set just above the top of the front mirror. The camera is adjusted so that some of the actual subject will show in the foreground in front of the reflected images.

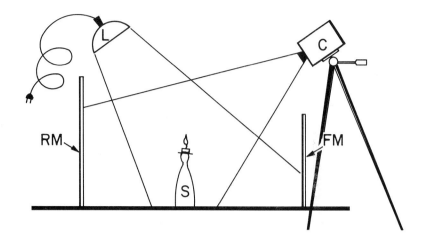

Fig. 3-12

Fig. 3-13

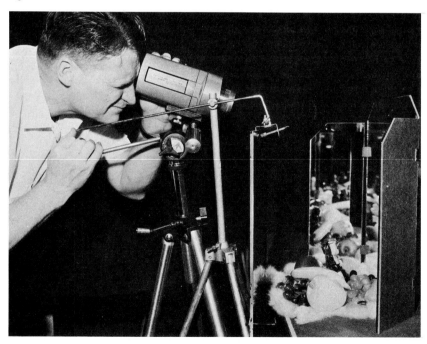

In Fig. 3-13 you see an actual setup, similar to the one in Fig. 3-12, but shown from a position just a little below and to the left of the light source. A tri-sectional mirror has been used (it stands easily by itself) in the position of the rear mirror in Fig. 3-12. Another, slightly shorter plain mirror is set on an artist's easel, and the author is making final, critical adjustments of camera,

Fig. 3-14a

Fig. 3-14b

Fig. 3-14c

tripod, and easel. Note how the thumb of the right hand is being used on the easel tilt-adjustment rod, which, in turn, is fastened to the top of the front mirror. The lens is also being zoomed, carefully and slowly, to observe different effects with different fields of view. Sometimes, with mirrors, minute changes will substantially alter the effects obtained. Just a few of the endless possibilities are shown in the following three scenes.

In Fig. 3-14a, a softer light, a larger lens opening, and focus set far forward — not on the actual figures but on the first reflected image — results in a pleasant overall treatment. Attention is concentrated on the one really clear point of focus, in the plane of the first set of images that appear to be facing the camera. The lighting would yield very pleasant, balanced color results.

In Fig. 3-14b the same point of focus is retained — on the first set of reflected images — but much brighter lighting was employed to enable a considerably smaller lens aperture to be used, increasing depth of field. The front mirror on the artist's easel was tilted slightly back toward the camera and turned slightly to one side. This resulted in a much longer line of images that seemed to mount a slight rise, the line of pilgrims curving around to the left a little as they went further back into the scene.

Figure 3-14c shows a less contrasty light being used for a softer effect. The point of focus has also been changed. This time the point of focus was actually on the *second* reflected image. Since the camera was focused at more distant points, the depth of field is also increased; here, the foreground and points far back into the reflections are all acceptably sharp. Thus, although the actual subject is less than two feet from the camera, the photographer is able to focus on a point almost four feet away by focusing on a *reflection* of the actual subject. It would be well to make a mental note of this fact — that is, that mirrors may be used to increase your depth of field by providing you with a more distant point of focus in reflected images. Although we are really studying the creation of multiple images at this stage, you may find this additional information of vital importance when, for instance, you may wish to film a subject that is very close to the camera but for which it would be beneficial to have a great depth of field.

Distance

Further note that in Figs. 3-14a, b, and c, the first reflected image faces you, the next does not, the following faces you, the next does not: so that the subject *alternates* facing you. This is because each successive mirrored image is reflected one more time so it is once more reversed.

Before we leave Fig. 3-14, take a careful look at the change of brightness of the subject matter as the images are repeated. The brightness of the images obviously decreases each time the image is reflected. The reason for this is that each time the image is again reflected, the light must travel an additional distance. This brings us to another law of light, one which you must know and remember if you are going to work with mirrors: *intensity of light varies inversely to the square of its distance from the source.* Thus the intensity of a light beam, or an image, which is simply a focused arrangement of light beams, will be one-fourth as strong when the beam (or image) travels twice the distance, one-ninth as strong when it travels three times as far, and so on. Each reflected image will be darker than the original subject and each image preceding it, due to the weakening of light intensity as the image travels a greater distance to the film plane. This variance in light intensity could become critical in color photography, especially if you are shooting the scene so all, or part, of the actual subject (as is the case in scenes of the pilgrim candles that we have just studied) is shown in the foreground. Light going directly from the subject to the camera travels the shortest possible distance to the film so light from the actual image is stronger than that from any of the reflected images. This difference in light intensity can be considerable in cases in which images are being reflected many times, or when the mirrors are placed far apart or far from the subject. In such cases, do what you can to avoid "washing out" the actual subject in the foreground by using less light on the side of the subject facing the camera and by using softer floodlighting rather than harsher spotlighting. Where possible, of course, avoid having the actual subject too close to the camera.

While the loss of light intensity with each reflected image creates some problems, it also can become a problem with a silver lining — if you'll pardon the pun. You can use this factor of light intensity loss and subsequent image-darkening to your advantage if you *want* your scenes to produce the effect of the images fading into the distance. The mirror is not a cure-all; it is the door to a great deal of photographic adventure, and like all doors, it opens onto some problems that are hard to overcome and others that just can't be eliminated. It

Fig. 3-15a

Fig. 3-15b

Fig. 3-15c

is your job to pick out the goodies: Use the mirror technique where it will solve a problem or really contribute to what you are trying to do, discard its use in situations that do not call for it or in which its use creates too many problems to make mirror-shooting practical.

The Effect of Water

Another favorite use for mirrors is to create the effect of water in a display or miniature set, such as the one shown in Fig. 3-15a. In this scene the photographer forgot to eliminate unwanted reflections of many things that were above and behind the set. While these were out of the camera's direct field of vision, the mirror "lake" was in a position to reflect them into the camera.

In Fig. 3-15b, the cameraman was most careful with his lights and concentrated them on the set alone. As a result, the background was so dark that it was not recorded in the lake. Another, even safer, procedure would have been to drape a black cloth background around the back of the set. It always pays to have an ample amount of black cloth around when working on scenes where reflection might become a problem. (I always keep about six yards on hand.)

In Fig. 3-15c, the cameraman has taken still another step to guard against unwanted reflections simply by lowering the shooting angle to a point where the foreground comes up into the picture far enough to cover the area of the lake that might show unwanted reflections. This also gives an added illusion of depth

69

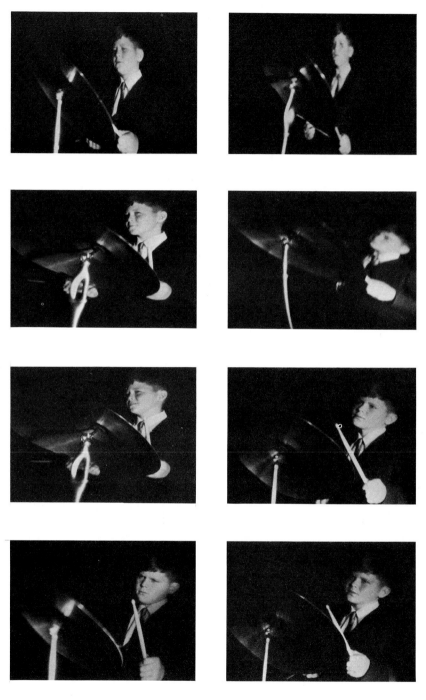

Fig. 3-16

Fig. 3-16

to the scene. With such a technique you must be careful to have enough light so that you may stop down and work with a small aperture, so that the foreground will be no more blurred than shown in this scene. It becomes unreal and objectionable if it is more out of focus than this. Again, remember that if you get into a jam and cannot get sufficient depth of focus, you might even enhance the reality of appearance by shooting with two mirrors (or one if you cannot make out lettering or numbers that would give the trick away) to enable you to get a greater depth of field. Shoot the reflected image of the whole scene.

Distorting Mirrors

Special distorting mirrors, such as those used in amusement parks, can be purchased, but they are expensive and hard to obtain in some areas. A flexible sheet of highly polished metal, such as a photographer's chromeplated ferrotype tin, is obtainable in most camera shops and can be used to make all sorts of distortions. All the pictures shown in Fig. 3-16 represent frames from a movie scene shot entirely from a large ferrotype tin. The subject was a rock-and-roll drummer against a black background (love that black cloth). The idea was that as the cymbal was hit and gave forth its CRASH the image of the drummer would become distorted and shimmer and waver. The various distortions were produced by bending the ferrotype tin from top to bottom or from side to side.

Don't forget, too, that you can scrape away the reflective coating on the rear side of a mirror and so create a number of special effects. Where there is clear glass (the areas from which the silver backing has been removed), the camera

71

will see through; yet it will record a reflection from the parts that remain silvered and reflective.

Furthermore, there are "see-through," or "two-way," mirrors that allow you to shoot from directly behind the mirror without the camera or cameraman being seen. Such mirrors are worth investigation and careful experimentation.

The world of mirrors is a fascinating one, and once you start your journey into it the possibilities are limited only by your enthusiasm, energy, and imagination. Look around you — a polished car fender or piece of chrome, a decorative convex mirror, one of the type used in stores to discourage shoplifting, a highly polished coffee pot — the list of odd shaped, highly reflective surfaces is endless, and so are your photographic possibilities using them.

4

Fog, Heat, Double Exposures, and Other Effects

There will be many times when you may wish to introduce a touch of the occult, or when some effect like fog or mist might transform a dull scene into one of special interest. You may even wish to include "ghosts" and other such film magic. It is not possible to create all such effects with ordinary or even quite expensive normal equipment, but this chapter will show you how to achieve a goodly number both easily and inexpensively and how to "get around" others.

Fog

If you were on vacation and came across something like the mothball fleet (which lies anchored in the Hudson River), you would want to film at least one or two scenes for historical record, if for no other reason. If it happened you arrived there on a bright, clear day, you'd have no trouble getting the clear factual shot shown in Fig. 4-1a. If you were fortunate enough to arrive in early morning and catch the fleet in an early morning haze (shown in Fig. 4-1b), you'd have a more interesting view. However, they could be used as the subject of a very interesting sequence if just a little simple "magic" were employed by the cameraman. There are many similar subjects you will come across in your travels. I'm using the mothball fleet as just one example.

For this subject, I'd suggest trying to arrive on the location on a clear summer day, at about 10 A.M., so that your opening scene might appear to have been shot at 8 or 9 A.M. when mist or fog would still not have been burnt off by the sun. Set your exposure "on the nose," as though you were going to shoot the scene without anything over your lens. Take a piece of chiffon cloth (extremely thin rayon or silk cloth) about 2′ x 2′ and hold it loosely in front of your lens. Lock the camera in the "on" position or have someone else run it. As the scene is being exposed, slowly and carefully move the cloth across the camera lens

73

Fig. 4-1a

Fig. 4-1b

Fig. 4-1c   Fig. 4-1d

allowing folds to form and unform. Take care that the cloth is always between the lens and the scene, and that it is moved not just straight across the lens but slightly up and down with the folds falling, mainly, horizontally across the lens. What you are trying to do is simulate the slow, lazy wafting of mist as it gradually rises and floats upward toward the camera. Figures 4-1c and 4-1d show two different frames from the same movie scene. You will note that the light and dark areas are slightly different in each frame. Thus, if these frames were projected one right after the other in a movie scene, the "fog" would drift and move. As you master this technique you will also learn to move the cloth slightly toward, then away from the camera.

I suggest that you make two exposures in addition to the "on-the-nose" exposure — one at one stop overexposed and the other two stops overexposed. These should be marked and used as tests. Once you have found a cloth and method of using it that most appeals to you, you will be able to make only one or two exposures to give you all the variety in exposure that you need to guarantee one good exposure. Until you are sure of your ground, however, make tests each time.

The cloth you use should be light, preferably white, as you do not wish to run the risk of coloring the fog or throwing off the color of your scene. Colored chiffon is fine if you are trying to show LSD hallucinations, other drug effects, or the fantasies of a saturated inebriate; otherwise, for natural fog, use white chiffon.

An excellent sequence could be made by starting out with a scene in which the fog seems to shroud the silent navy. Then at the end of the fog scene, slowly throw your lens completely out of focus while the camera is running. For the following scene, assume a different angle, either by moving the camera or by zooming in. Gradually bring the lens into focus, after removing the cloth. Another possibility is to zoom in a little closer at the end of the fog scene and throw the lens increasingly out of focus as you zoom. Then, when the next scene came into focus as it progressed, the transition from foggy to clear scenes would be quite natural. Either way, you wish to move in closer for at least two or three scenes so you may get a more detailed view of a small group of the vessels, then of a particular ship, then of a part or parts of interest, or of a special activity. Your choice would depend upon what you are attempting to "see" and what you wish to show your audience.

Fig. 4-2c

Fig. 4-2a   Fig. 4-2b

The technique of producing fog effects described here works equally well with still and videotape cameras. With the still camera, bear in mind that if you use too fast an exposure and stop down very far, you may register the cloth (though it is extremely fine-textured) just a little too clearly. If there is no rapid action in the scene, do not use a faster exposure than about 1/30 sec. In fact, if using a still camera or movie camera that permits very slow shutter speeds, you might be able to enhance the effect by using a 1/5-sec. or a 1/10-sec. exposure. This slower exposure might require the use of neutral density filter (which cuts down light intensity so that you can use slower exposures without stopping down to extremely small apertures) or a polarizing filter. This is another area in which experimentation will pay great dividends.

What I am going to talk about now might well be classified under filter and prism effects, but since it is so closely related to what we have just covered, I wish to discuss it while we are on the subject of artificial fog and mist. There are such things as fog filters. If you ask for them in your local camera shop, they may not have them in stock but I am sure they can procure them for you — once you get the clerk to understand that you wish to induce fog, not eliminate it. When you ask for a fog filter, the average response will be to show you a light-orange-tinted or similar filter designed to cut down atmospheric haze. The "fog" filter you want is colorless and, when held up to the light, will look as though you had captured a little extremely fine mist in the glass. You can get these fog filters in various densities. I would suggest you start with the heavy fog effect type.

On a visit to the quaint and beautifully restored town of Old Mystic, Conn., I was confronted with the lighting shown in Fig. 4-2a — fine for good, even color and detail work (when I moved in closer with my motion-picture and still cameras) and great for a clear departing shot. But, for the introductory scene to any place named "Old Mystic," this lighting hardly seemed appropriate. Just by putting a heavy fog filter over the lens, I was able to conjure up the soft, misty scene in Fig. 4-2b, much more fitting for the introduction to this remnant of our historical past. You could further add to the effect by utilizing the thin chiffon discussed above in conjunction with the fog filter. You may also make your own fog filter by simply stretching thin white chiffon tight across an adapter ring and fastening it so that the whole device can be screwed in place over the lens. This homemade filter gives an overall mist without the rolling effect of the commercial fog filter. You may use more than one thickness of cloth if you want especially severe fog effects. You may also mount stretched cloth between two pieces of circular clear glass, and fit and glue this assembly into an adapter ring of proper size to make your own filter. Flashlight replacement lenses of clear, round, flat glass are good for this construction.

The chiffon may also be mounted on an artist's canvas-stretching frame or a sewing hoop and held in front of the lens. You can also treat a flashlight replacement lens with an airbrush in light mist-gray paint in slightly varying densities to simulate rolling fog. Such a coated lens, if mounted in a proper adapter ring, could be slowly rotated while shooting to simulate the movement of fog or mist. We have but scratched the surface of the possibilities. Explore and discover the many, many effects you can create.

Once you have introduced a mystical setting such as this, you can then introduce some effect — a wipe, fade, or out-of-focus and back-to-focus technique — to move from the mystical to the clear. You can then show beautiful clear renditions of various scenes within such quaint areas as may be seen in Figs. 4-2c, 4-2d, and 4-2e. Such "following" scenes give you ample opportunity to include explanatory narration and/or captions, titles, and so on.

In Fig. 4-3a we see a large sailing vessel preparing to depart a small cove in a miniature model set. This is the type of scene that would lend itself to some additional atmosphere. By letting some light fall on the fine white chiffon, as we slowly wave it loosely in front of the camera lens, we build up even more light on the folds so they appear as denser segments of fog. The effect is shown in Fig. 4-3b. On the other hand, if we take the same cloth and stretch it tight, we will get the rather uniform misty effect seen in Fig. 4-3c.

Fig. 4-2d

Fig. 4-2e

Shooting Through Water

All sorts of interesting effects can be obtained by filling a small glass fish tank with clear water. Make sure the glass is spotless inside and out. Shoot any scene through the glass and water. Care should be taken, of course, to make certain the sides, the surface of the water, and the base of the tank do not show.

A matte box should be used as a sunshade in front of the camera to prevent the lens from being reflected into the glass in front of it. A black cloth is draped

78

Fig. 4-3a   Fig. 4-3b

Fig. 4-3c

over the shiny parts of the matte box guides and the aluminum tripod, to prevent these parts from being reflected off the glass. The matte box is brought up close to the tank. The actual distance will be determined by the size of the aquarium and how "in focus" you wish the effects to be. In Fig. 4-4b the lens is focused on the desert scene beyond the fish tank. The actual scene is illuminated just as though the aquarium were not between the camera lens and it. However, when you take your exposure readings through the glass, be most careful to aim the meter so it will see the scene at the same angle and same direction as the camera lens. The Bell & Howell shown has a built-in Optronic Eye exposure control, which automatically sets the exposure. In this case the automatic through-the-lens exposure control is very helpful. If you wish to vary your exposure effects, this camera and certain others like it have an override that allows you to turn off the control that sets the lens aperture automatically. Thus you fix your lens manually at any aperture you wish. The field of vision of the lens should be far enough below the surface of the water so that it will not see the disturbance caused by the impact of coloring being dropped into the water.

In Fig. 4-4a, red food coloring has been dropped into the water in line with the lens so that as it descends and spreads out, it will appear before the camera lens. The way this effect develops is shown by movie frames 4-4b, 4-4c, 4-4d, 4-4e, and 4-4f. The food coloring, being slightly heavier than the water, will drift slowly downward. As more and more food coloring is added, the clouding effect will become more dense and can be made to appear to

Fig. 4-4a

Fig. 4-4b

Fig. 4-4c

Fig. 4-4d

Fig. 4-4e

Fig. 4-4f

envelop a whole scene or a title. Remember, this is red and in color it would be most dramatic. You may even add other food colors so that the clouds will change colors. You may carefully agitate the water from one side, out of sight of the lens, and cause the coloring to swirl around, finally fading into the whole area. This would result in a scene that looks as though it had been shot through a series of different-colored filters. You may also drop other liquids or detergents into the water for still other effects. Dropping Alka-Seltzer tablets into the water will cause bubbles to rise in front of the lens. The possibilities are endless with this simple setup.

You can shoot outdoor and long-distance indoor scenes through such an aquarium. If you want the appearance of a rainstorm, you can shoot through

80

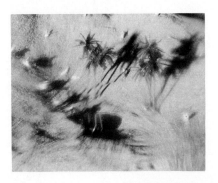
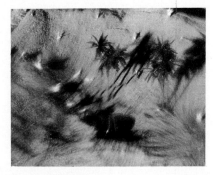

Fig. 4-5a   Fig. 4-5b

Fig. 4-5c

the aquarium while a helper pours water into it from a sprinkling can. In this case, the aquarium provides a convenient means of keeping the water from spilling all over while you are exposing the scene. If you wish to convey the idea you are shooting through a window pane, you can allow some of the sprinkling to fall directly on the inside of the aquarium facing the camera. The "raindrops" will start streaking down the "pane." Naturally, if the scene is to run long, you must make arrangements for "rain" in lifelike proportion to the set or actual subject, to fall on set or subject. If, for instance, it is supposed to be raining on a miniature set, you would employ a fine mist over the area of the set. The sprinkler can be used close to the camera, because raindrops close to the camera are quite large in proportion to the distant rain, even in real life.

Desert Heat

Other effects might be called for in a scene like the desert set. To show intense heat, for example, frames as in Figs. 4-5a, 4-5b, 4-5c when projected will produce a shimmering heat wave. Out-of-focus and in-focus areas were produced by spreading vaseline very thinly on some areas of a clear piece of glass for the out-of-focus areas and by leaving it off, or almost off, for the in-focus areas. It is surprising how little vaseline it takes to create the distortion,

81

so remember to spread it very thinly. The vaseline-coated glass is then slipped into the grooved retainers of the matte box in front of the camera lens. Depending upon the effect you want, you would put the glass slide in the retainers in either the front or the rear of the matte box. I prefer to work with the vaseline-coated glass or heavy acetate in the large opening, which may be set farthest from the camera lens. This allows me to move the glass slide toward and away from the lens, as the camera is shooting the scene, to add to the illusion of the distortion being caused by intense heat waves. Another use to which this device can be put is when the camera sees what an actor is seeing when the actor, caught in the desert, is beginning to lose consciousness.

If you do not have a matte box or another convenient way of moving the vaseline-coated slide smoothly toward and away from the lens, you may achieve a similar effect by using several acetate or glass disks, each one coated a little differently from the others. These disks should fit snugly inside a filter holder. You could then single-frame the scene, making a series of single frame shots each with a different disk in place and some with the same glass turned at a slightly different position to the lens, by rotating. What you should do is place the completely and almost completely clear areas of vaseline-smeared glass in different positions in front of the lens as each frame is shot, so that this slight, controlled variation will appear as a natural wavering when the film is projected. As with all of this type of work, you must shoot tests with your equipment. When doing so, carefully "slate" the start of each scene — that is, shoot about a second of footage of a board on which is written the essential information (f/stop, frames per second, focal length of lens, etc.) together with identifying scene and "take" numbers. This way, when you see the scene projected, you will know definitely what you have done, how you did it, and what effect it had.

The heat wave effect is one that is often combined with the out-of-focus–back-into-focus technique. Often the focus is varied only slightly in and out as the heat wave starts to occur. Then as the scene proceeds and the heat effect is made more pronounced, the in-and-out-of-focus may also be more extreme. What you must guard against is indulging in too extreme an effect for too long a period or at the wrong times. You know the scene will have to run a while longer, but you also know that the scene must be intelligible and must still communicate with some degree of clarity to your audience. The extreme, when the scene becomes a complete blur, must be reserved for the climax of the scene — approximately the last 6 inches in 16mm and 3 inches in 8mm (about $1\frac{1}{2}$ sec. on videotape). There is no hard-and-fast rule regarding tempo, effects, and so on. You must develop a feel for proper scene, effect, and length. This comes only with practice. Whatever you do, try to look at your films as a stranger would. Be objective, not indulgent. Again, the key is to keep uppermost in your mind that the special effect is not the subject of your scene — it is the window-dressing and should be used only to the extent that it contributes to appropriate presentation of the subject. Rarely can you allow the effect to dominate except in either the opening or closing part of the scene. For instance, if the subject's vision is supposed to be clearing, you could start with a distortion effect at the head of the scene and show more clearing of vision as the scene progresses. If, on the other hand, vision of the subject is supposed to be more and more affected, then acute, or total, distortion would take place at the tail end of the scene.

If you are making still pictures, you have to be even more careful in regard to the distortion. Normally you would have to use at least two shots, one to show the scene without the heat wave effect and one to show the scene with the effect. In a still picture sequence or picture story, the effect could hardly ever reach the extreme stages permissible in movies or videotapes. In a still picture, considerable finesse is necessary, and the extent to which the distortion can be utilized is much more subtle to decide. A complete blur-out, for instance, would mean nothing, as there would be no preceding frames to ease the mind of the audience through the beginning of scene distortion. Maximum distortion in a still picture should probably be no more than that shown in Fig. 4-5a. The scene still communicates ample distortion, but you should never go further than this in still photography.

Shooting Through Smoke

All sorts of cloud and fog effects may be created by shooting through actual smoke. Outdoors and on large sets you may wish to employ some type

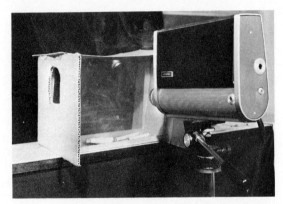

Fig. 4-6a

Fig. 4-6b

of commercial smokebomb. I imagine you would have no trouble procuring such items from theatrical supply companies or fireworks manufacturers. However, beginning this type of photography requires no more than a few cigarettes, some corrugated cardboard, two panes of picture-frame glass, and some black electrical tape. In Figs. 4-6a and 4-6b a very crude setup is shown. Since my Ampex Videotape camera has a 1-inch (25mm) lens, I used it to check some effects first. Having a 25mm lens means that the result at any given aperture would compare with the results that would be obtained with the standard lens for 16mm cameras. There would, of course, be even greater depth of field with 8mm and Super 8mm camera "standard" lenses, which are often 15mm and under (about half the focal length of their counterpart in 16mm lenses). The shorter the focal length, the greater the depth of field. Thus, I knew that with the Ampex Videotape camera I would get effects less in focus for any particular lens setting than with a Super 8mm or 8mm camera. They would, of course, be more in focus than with the standard lens on a 35mm camera, which would have a focal length of about 50mm (approximately 2 inches).

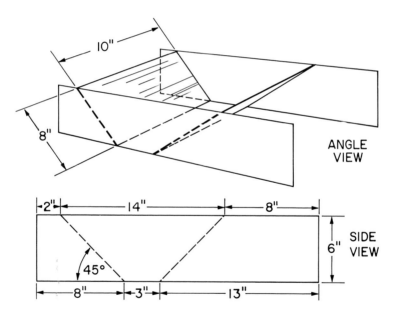

Fig. 4-7

In Fig. 4-6a, note the amount of smoke build-up in the glass-enclosed compartment in front of the camera, caused by simply placing a shirt cardboard over the open top of the chamber. In addition to needing a build-up in quantity of smoke, you need light shining on the fumes in order for them to show up well on the film. Smoke filmed against a black background would not register

84

any image if it were not lighted. The rough hole cut in the cardboard at left provides the necessary light. Note how bright the cardboard is. This is because a strong light was directed on the cardboard side, centered on the hole there. In Fig. 4-6b, I have turned off this side, smoke-illuminating light and have just begun to remove the shirt cardboard. As you can see, even though the smoke has not had time to clear, it is almost invisible both inside and outside the enclosure.

Note, also, that in Fig. 4-6a there is a definite lens reflection in the glass facing the camera. Remembering one of the laws of light (the angle of incidence is equal to the angle of reflection), you will realize that by tilting the glass at about a 45-degree angle to the base of the smoke chamber and, consequently, at a 45-degree angle to the lens and the perpendicular of the film plane, any image that might form on the glass panes will be reflected away from the camera lens. This would hold true of both panes of glass since, actually, the one nearest the lens would be tilted about 45 degrees downward and the pane opposite would be tilted about 45 degrees upward in relation to the camera lens.

It is suggested that you conduct your own experiments with a crude, easy-to-change setup, such as shown. As a helpful guide, however, Fig. 4-7 has also been included. One-fourth-inch plywood suffices nicely. All the material you need to make this setup can be cut from one piece of 1/4-inch thick plywood 24" x 18". Cut the pieces as follows: one piece 1/4" x 3" x 10" for the bottom; and two pieces, each 1/4" x 6" x 24", for the sides. You will also need two panes of picture-frame glass, each 8" x 10". Use 1"-wide black electrical plastic tape to make all joinings and to hold everything stable. Before assembling the setup, paint all surfaces of the wood flat black in order to cut down any possibility of reflection. You may make a "lid" by using a piece of cardboard or another piece of plywood 12" x 18". This should be a little larger than the smoke compartment, the top of which measures about 10" x 14". Paint the lid flat black on both sides and on all edges — the underside is the only part that must be black but you might as well make it look good. The sketch in Fig. 4-7 is self-explanatory. You should have no trouble following it.

From Dr. Jekyll to Mr. Hyde

The smoke chamber has many uses. One is shown in the Dr. Jekyll-Mr. Hyde sequence. Pouring the drink (Fig. 4-8a) and drinking the concoction (Fig. 4-8b) are shot without any smoke in the chamber. Figure 4-8c shows the start of the transformation and was shot through smoke. At this point, three or four cigarettes have been lit and placed in a suitable ash tray or dish, which is placed in the center of the chamber on its base. Since you still wish only a slight smoke effect, hardly visible, the lid has not been put on top of the smoke chamber. In Fig. 4-8d, the lid has been put in place and the smoke, prevented from escaping out of the top of the chamber, starts to swirl around and build up in the compartment. In Fig. 4-8e, the smoke has become quite dense, and through the swirling smoke a different face starts to become visible. In Fig. 4-8f, another glimpse is caught of the monster's face as the smoke whirls

Fig. 4-8a

Fig. 4-8b

Fig. 4-8c

Fig. 4-8d

around. Figures 4-8g, 4-8h, and 4-8i represent shots made through the swirling smoke. These shots represent just random frames selected from within the scene. The transition would actually take many more frames.

To heighten the effect, you can zoom in slightly and then slowly zoom back out during the scene. You can also rotate the lens slightly in and out of focus as the transformation is taking place. Care must be taken, however, that all of this is done slowly enough so as not to distort beyond comprehension what is taking place. You want your audience to become aware that a definite change is happening.

At the close of the scene, remove the lid of the chamber and allow the smoke to escape while still shooting. The air will clear and, as it does, the monstrous face will become clear and the audience will be hit with the full impact of the transformation. Figs. 4-8j and 4-8k show the end of the sequence.

Equipment and Tests

Between the smoke chamber just shown and the use of food coloring and other liquids in the fish tank you have an excellent range of special effects useful for transitions, creating your own weather effects, title embellishment and changes, time lapses, and many other adaptations. The smoke effects just shown in Fig. 4-8 were stills made with a 35mm still camera with a 50mm lens. A standard 16mm lens or the standard 8mm one would render even more

Fig. 4-8e

Fig. 4-8f

Fig. 4-8g

Fig. 4-8h

Fig. 4-8i

Fig. 4-8j

Fig. 4-8k

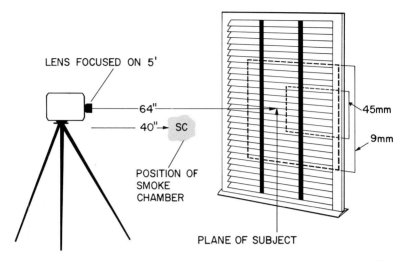

LENS FOCUSED ON 5'

64"

40"→ SC

POSITION OF
SMOKE
CHAMBER

45mm

9mm

PLANE OF SUBJECT

Fig. 4-9

definite smoke swirls because of their greater depth of field and sharper rendition of the smoke itself, even though the same stop were used. The camera was focused on the subject, which was placed slightly behind the smoke chamber. As stated above, depth of field for any lens may be increased by focusing on a more distant point.

The distance you would be able to move the camera back from the smoke chamber would, of course, depend upon two things; the size of the glass panes used and the focal length of the lens. Since shorter focal lengths provide wider angles and longer focal lengths (which give a much narrower field of view) have less depth of field, if you wish more depth of field, it would be easiest to use larger panes of glass and place the smoke chamber farther from the camera. This is especially true of 4" x 5" cameras, such as the professional Speed Graphic or view cameras. The normal focal-length lens for these cameras is about 127mm. However, as you get into shorter and shorter focal-length lenses, you acquire increasing latitude due to the increased depth of field. The standard lens for the 35mm camera is about 50mm; for 16mm and many standard videotape cameras, it is about 25mm; for 8mm and Super 8mm, it goes down to 15mm and lower. Thus, by the time you get down to the 8mm cameras, your choices are very wide, provided there is a way of checking focus and field of vision on your camera, for any given aperture and distance setting. Figure 4-9 shows a simple method of checking the size of the glass panes you need when working at your most common aperture or the largest aperture you would want to use on your camera. I made some rough tests with my Bell & Howell Super 8mm Focustronic movie camera. This camera has a zoom lens that will go all the way from 9mm to 45mm, so I decided to test it at the extremes.

In making this test you should use a window, preferably one with a venetian blind, so that you can easily determine the field of vision by counting the slats of the blind that you can see in your viewfinder and by checking over from the blind tapes to the edge of window. If you do not have such a window, you may use an extremely large cardboard and have someone mark on it the edges of your field of vision at sides, top, and bottom of your viewfinder. You will also need a doll, a tray with some design, or some other object on which you will be able to determine the approximate degree of focus when you set it in the foreground. The window was used to represent the plane in which my subject would be placed; the tray indicates the smoke in the smoke chamber. We are attempting to determine how clear the smoke would be when the camera is focused on a subject set beyond the chamber so that we may determine how large the two panes of glass should be.

With the lens set on its fullest "telephoto" position — giving it a focal length of 45mm — the camera was placed 64 inches from the subject (the window). The tray (representing the center of the smoke chamber) was placed 40 inches from the camera. The focus was on 60 inches. In order to make the test for one of the largest apertures (the shortest depth of field), I used an aperture of $f/2$. Now, remember, in the case of smoke, we do not have to test for absolute sharpness since smoke does not have to be shown with needle-sharp clarity. At $f/2$, we want an acceptable degree of clarity as opposed to a vague rendition. In this simple test I found that the field of vision in this camera at the 45mm (full telephoto) setting was about 6 inches vertically and 8 inches horizontally. Since the smoke chamber would be placed 14 inches closer to the camera (at the point where the tray was located) than the window on which the 6″ x 8″ scene was measured, I could be sure that 8″ x 10″ glass panes, even though slanted at 45 degrees (see Fig. 4-6b), would provide 10 inches in width and 6 inches in height. Since the chamber would be 14 inches closer than the window, I could still be sure that the cigarettes would be below the camera lens and would not show in the picture. You do not lose anything in width when you slant the glass panes, but you do lose about 25 per cent of the height.

At the extreme wide-angle setting of only 9mm, I found that the field of vision on the window was about 28 inches in height and 38 inches in width. Remember that you lose about 25 per cent in height when you build the smoke chamber and slant the glass panes at 45-degree angles. Another thing to remember that will speed up your arithmetic is that 25 per cent off is also 75 per cent on. So just multiply 28″ x 0.75, and you will get the same answer: if the *actual* height of a pane of glass is 28 inches, when it is slanted at a 45-degree angle, it will appear to be 21 inches high.

Also bear in mind that glass panes can usually be most easily obtained in standard sizes, which often run in multiples of 1 foot. To allow room for the cigarettes to be out of sight at the base of the chamber, you will not want less than an effective height of approximately 28 inches after the panes of glass are installed, slanted at a 45-degree angle. If you multiply 36 inches by 0.75, you get a working height of 27 inches. Because 36 inches is an easier size to obtain at a reasonable price, I suggest, in this case, that the cameraman try to work with panes of glass measuring 36″ x 36″ or the next size larger in a standard cut stock. It should be noted at this point though that the smaller the chamber, the fewer cigarettes or other smoke-producers will be needed in order to produce dense smoke effects easily. It is suggested you start with a small chamber utilizing 8″ x 10″ glass, as shown in Fig. 4-6b. When you are thoroughly familiar with the techniques involved and are in a better position to determine just what size for the final chamber would suit most of your purposes, then make the larger chamber.

Although I found cigarettes to be one of the simplest and most efficient smoke-generators, you can also get smoke pills and smoke liquid at hobby shops. They are used in model railroad locomotives to produce smoke from the funnels while they are running. There is a heating coil in the funnel of such locomotives and this makes the pill or liquid smoke. In using this type of smoke-making pill or liquid, you have to devise some other method of generating enough heat to cause the pills or liquid to turn to smoke.

Never overlook the possibility of combining tricks you have learned. For instance, you can use a fog-inducing filter or cloth over your lens and, simultaneously, shoot through the smoke chamber to create moving segments of mist and fog. The most interesting and rewarding part of trick photography is always the way you use your knowledge to work things out for yourself. It allows you a tremendous spectrum of creativity and originality in spite of all that has been done before.

Double Exposures

One thing I regret about most 35mm still as well as the Super 8mm movie cameras is their inability to double-expose. This comes under the heading of You Can't Have Everything. There is no denying that the cartridge-loading Super 8mm or instamatic load cameras avoid a great deal of edge-fogging, and make loading simple and fast. The excellent quick transport device on 35mm still cameras, such as the Canon Pellix, which transports the film and cocks the shutter in one swift movement, is certainly an indispensable feature if you want to shoot a quick succession of still pictures with speed and convenience. This is needed far more frequently than a way of making double exposures. Some 35mm still cameras, such as the Canon Pellix, have a way in which the film can be wound back to any particular frame and as many exposures as are desired can be made. To get the frame exactly in line with the way it was in each preceding exposure, however, requires great care. In making double exposures with still cameras, the film should remain stationary between exposures so you can be sure of the exact position of the film in each exposure. For this reason I use my 4″ x 5″ Speed Graphic and cutfilm holders for making most double exposures. I can later reshoot the resultant picture or transparency even for use as a movie scene, provided the scene does not have to show moving-picture action. The photos in Figs. 4-10, 4-11, and 4-12 were all made this way by the 4″ x 5″ camera using cutfilm holders. Figure 4-10 shows triple exposures, each set of three being made on one piece of 4″ x 5″ cut film. Black is the best background for multiple exposures because it will never conflict with the subject image. The only areas in which the subject will appear transparent are those areas in which the subject overlaps itself.

A simple method of using any 35mm still camera to obtain a double exposure effect (as long as motion is not going to appear in the scene) is to shoot

Fig. 4-10

Fig. 4-11a

Fig. 4-12

Fig. 4-11b

two different frames, one after the other. In the first scene the subject would appear on the right side of the picture. In the second one the subject would appear on the left side of the picture. The camera should not be moved, of course. You want to obtain two identical pictures, except that in one the subject is on the right and in the other the subject is on the left. Have the negatives developed as slides. Remove the two "identical" frames from their slide holders. Place one on top of the other, both with the emulsion side down, shiny side up, so that the scenes match up exactly, one over the other. They have to be held firmly in exact register, while you cut with one sure stroke through both slides at the same time, right down the center. Use a fresh, single-edge razor blade for the cutting. Discard the halves having no subject in them. Carefully place the two remaining halves, each of which do have the subject in them together, so that each half lines up exactly with the other and the background runs from one half to the other as though there were no break. Cement these halves in place between two pieces of thin glass the size of the 35mm slide so that the film lies perfectly flat. There should be no line of

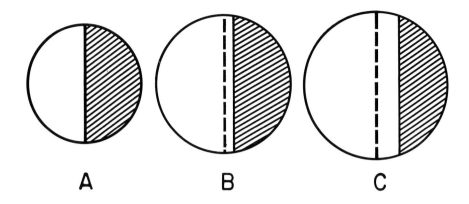

Fig. 4-13

light at the joint in the center of the picture when the slide is projected. You can then copy the projected vision of the whole scene with either a still or a movie camera and get a final composite scene.

Up to this point in our discussion we have overlooked a fundamental requirement for this kind of work — that of utilizing a matte box or some type of mask in front of the film or lens. In most cases you will have to be content with a masking device in front of the lens. The following is the method. Figure 4-13 shows how the sizes of the masks may proportionately vary: A is exactly half the lens area, B just slightly more than half the lens area, and C about two-thirds the lens area. C was the type of mask used over the 127mm lens on the 4″ x 5″ camera used to make the photos in Figs. 4-10, 4-11a, and 4-12. The dotted line shows the actual center of the lens, while the shaded area represents the segment cut out of the mask, the area through which the light from the scene will pass to expose the picture. The white area is the size of the mask.

Masks may be cut from black construction paper available in almost any stationery store. They should be fixed into a filter ring so they will not fall out and will turn when the ring is turned. You should expose one side of the film with the mask set as shown. Then rotate the ring so that the open portion of the mask is on the opposite side for the next exposure. The reason why the mask should overlap the center of the lens this much on a 4″ x 5″ camera is that the 127mm lens, not having as much depth of field as lenses for 8mm and other cameras, would see the mask only as a vague dividing point and would, therefore, allow a lot of light-spill around its actual edge. If you used a mask like A, even though you made it large enough to split the actual lens exactly in half, you would end up with the center section of your picture overexposed. Too much light would bleed over from each masked half in each of the two single exposures made on the one piece of film. Make tests for your own equipment. The size and proportion of the mask will vary with both the focal length of your lens and the aperture being used (closing down increases your

Fig. 4-14a   Fig. 4-14b

depth of field). When you find the ideal proportions for each aperture, indicate on that mask the size aperture for which it best works. In this way, any time you wish to work at a particular lens stop, you will know which mask is best for it.

There are some 8mm and 16mm cameras designed to be used for making double exposures and many other effects. Some of these even allow a slide to be inserted in front of the film so that the slide or mask is very close to the film itself. This means that a precise masking of any area of the film may be achieved easily. Since very few readers will have such equipment, I will not go into use of it here. Besides, the owner's manual for such equipment covers use related to special effects quite thoroughly and with direct reference to the specific equipment. If you are interested in this kind of equipment, contact Bolex (Paillard), Bell & Howell, Eastman Kodak, and other leading firms, describing precisely the types of effects you wish to do in the camera. Ask what they have available in cameras using the size film with which you prefer to work. If they have nothing of the type you describe, ask them to tell you to whom you might write for further information. Big-name firms such as these are quite helpful and will be glad to answer your questions.

There is, of course, a professional way to produce a double-exposure effect with an ordinary movie camera. This involves making two series of identical scenes (except for subject placement) and having them printed in combination at an optical printing laboratory. Before shooting, check with the labs to find out what film size they handle. With 16mm you should have no problem, because 16mm is an accepted professional size now. Super 8mm and 8mm may be difficult to get processed, however.

When you have a situation involving movement, you have the additional problem of synchronizing action. Take the example of the two chess players (actually the same person playing against himself) in Fig. 4-14. This type of scene involves the movement of chess pieces. While one player is making a move, the other player will have to be present — that is, both players must end up being in the entire scene. What you wish to obtain then is two sets of scenes that run the same length and time which, when combined into one scene through optical printing, will result in proper dovetailing of action.

For this type of work you must have a strong tripod to hold your camera rigidly in place. You will want everything along the joining point to match from one side to the other. A script for shooting the "first" scene would actually be a script for two scenes:

SCENE 1A: Chess player on right with white pieces makes first move. Looks at chessboard briefly (3 seconds). After exactly 3 seconds, makes a move. At total 4½ seconds move must be completed. Let scene run to end (total for 9 seconds for whole scene) while subject looks across table to where opponent will be seated.

SCENE 1B: Chess player, now seated on left with black pieces, is looking at chessboard. After exactly 3 seconds, looks up at opponent who would then be starting to make his move. At 3½ seconds, player on left looks back down at chessboard, and at 4½ seconds looks like he is deciding on his move. At exactly 7 seconds, player on left makes his move, which must be completed not later than 8½ seconds (to give some margin before scene is stopped at exactly 9 seconds).

If we compare what we have now shot on a chart it would line up as follows:

Length of Time Scene Has Run	Action in Scene 1A	Action in Scene 1B
0 sec.–3 sec.	Player on right looks at chessboard	Player on left looks at board
3 sec.–4½ sec.	Player on right moves piece	Player on left looks at opponent, then down at board
4½ sec.–7 sec.	Player on right settles back watching board and opponent	Player on left considers move, starts it at exactly 7 sec.
7 sec.–8½ sec.	Player watches opponent making move	Player on left makes his move, completes not later than 8½ sec.
8½ sec.–9 sec.	Both players watch chessboard	

When the optical printing laboratory gets these two scenes, with the proper instructions, the right half of Scene 1A will be used with the left half of Scene 1B. Thus you would end up with one scene, a total of 9 seconds long, in which the player on the right would make the first move, and the player on the left would make the second move.

To continue with the illusion that the player is playing against himself, you can cut down considerably on the number of scenes in which the two players are actually shown together by using various subterfuges. You may move in for a close shot of a hand making a move so that you do not have to show the people involved. You may move to a close-up of the face of one player as he either makes a move or watches the opponent make one, but just showing the player alone, looking in the proper direction. If someone looks reasonably like the player from either side or from the back, you may shoot over the shoulder of the look-alike, showing the actual front face of only one player.

Spaced sparingly between such shots, you should use scenes showing both players to keep the audience convinced that two people, identical to each other, really are playing each other. The point is you do not have to prove your point in *each shot,* just prove it occasionally enough to be convincing.

It is, of course, important to use good motion-picture equipment with a high-quality intermittent movement — the mechanism used to transport the film through the camera — when you are attempting to combine scenes. An aid in this respect is not to use backgrounds with too much detail in them, especially in the area where the two scenes will be joined (usually at center). The same would hold true for superimposing an image over a background. I would suggest, in any case in which you were going to superimpose an image, that you shoot the image to be superimposed against a black background whenever possible. This completely avoids the problem of matching backgrounds.

The Glass-Shot

There is a very simple and effective method of superimposing a title, ghost, or scene that can be utilized with any camera; it requires no double exposure, no winding back, and so on. This is done by using what is commonly called a "glass-shot."

The easiest use of this technique involves shooting an image that is being reflected off a piece of ordinary glass, usually set at about 45 degrees to the optical axis of the lens, the idea being to create a ghost effect. Most effective results are obtained by setting the ghost against a black background and lighting your phantom so that it will be a weaker image than your main scene: you want it to appear transparent. A good way to check your results beforehand is to use a Polaroid camera — or, if you have such a setup, a videotape camera — making some trial shots to determine accurately the actual effect on film before you put it on your movie or still film. Of course, exposure balance between actual scene and phantom should be carefully checked with an accurate external meter (such as the Weston Ranger 9). Once you learn the proper exposure relationship for the film you are using in terms of careful meter readings, few, if any, test shots will be necessary to obtain excellent results.

The Two-Way Mirror

A two-way mirror is another excellent tool in making trick shots of this nature. While you can look through the mirror to the scene beyond, an image will also be reflected from the front surface of such a mirror. Again, there is the question of light balance. You have to decide how weak, how transparent, or how "solid" (in the case of a superimposed title) you wish the reflected image to appear.

If you are willing to experiment, your results can be most rewarding and your accomplishments without limit. Just to mention a passing idea: suppose you wanted to have a scene magically appear behind your subject, for example, a Christmas scene. You could put a two-way mirror in the doorway of a room in which the Christmas scene was set up. This should be done at night, when darkening the room completely could be accomplished simply by turning off the lights. You can have your subject sit so his image is reflected into the camera from the front of the two-way mirror. You would probably shoot a head-and-shoulders medium close-up of the subject or a close-up head shot (to keep down the size of your two-way mirror). If you get too far back, you'd have to buy a larger mirror, and this could be quite expensive. Try to get just far enough from the mirror to stop down sufficiently so that the scene in the room will be clear when it appears. Have the lights arranged in the room so that they may be turned on one by one to make the scene gradually brighter or turned up brighter together. Shoot about two seconds of the reflection of the subject alone. Then have someone turn on the lights one at a time. Your helper should not be shown doing this. You may have to stop your camera to let him change position each time a light is turned on. If you can have the lights wired so they can be remote-controlled, or if all of them will work off a control that will allow you to increase their intensity gradually, it is best not to stop the camera. Many cameras will not start exactly on-speed and the first frame or frames may be exposed differently each time you start. These off-color frames would have to be cut out later.

What will happen with this setup is that the scene in the room beyond the two-way mirror will not show at all until you start turning on the lights. With each increase in illumination, or as the lights are all increased in intensity, the scene will come through the two-way mirror more and more. As the scene in the room becomes quite strong, the subject may move out of the way so only the room beyond the mirror will show. Toward the end of the scene you may zoom in closer to the interior of the room beyond the mirror. You then will be all set to shoot additional scenes directly with the mirror out of the way. This and other similar tricks can be most effective in adding professionalism and interest to your work.

5

Backgrounds

Photography is a field of such never-ending exploration and adventure that all you really need at first, given a particular interest and amount of equipment, are kernels of knowledge to start you on your own experimentation. It is far more important for you to learn well that which you can do most simply, within a comparatively modest budget, than for you to become a walking fountainhead of advanced data on how Hollywood achieves its results on million-dollar films. You learn best what you learn by doing yourself. This is as true of backgrounds as it is of the other areas we have covered thus far.

The first thing you probably think in regard to artificial backgrounds is the field of back-projection. While it is entirely possible to project a background large enough for you to shoot life-size movies in front of it, the equipment involved is most costly. Because projection onto such large background areas requires the projectors to be placed far from the background screen, the light intensity on the screen falls off, even with wide-angle or zoom projection lenses. To compensate for this, professionals use bright arc lamps in the projectors, which often require current in the 200 amp. range. Even a well-wired house should not be loaded over 30 amp. on any one fuse, and it is often advisable to keep the amperage requirement around 20 amp. If you have professional work to do that requires large-size projected backgrounds, the best advice I can give you is to rent the equipment necessary from a firm that also provides transportation for it, as well as operators who know how to operate the equipment and tie it into electrical sources. In short, if you are lucky enough to be commissioned to do a film for pay, arrange to subcontract background projected scenes *before* setting a price on a film incorporating such effects. In this way, you will avoid bankruptcy, burning down studios or houses, and cremating personnel. Besides, the best possible education you could get in the field of advanced background projection may be obtained by hiring a reliable group of such specialists and working with them. There are tricks to every trade and these specialists know the best ones. Until you can get this kind of assistance, however, there is much to be accomplished, with basic equipment, in even the homiest surroundings.

Stills and Paintings as Backgrounds

The easiest background for the beginner to use is the painted or photographed backdrop. It is an area not part of the live action or set, in the foreground, but a still placed somewhere in the area to the rear of the subject.

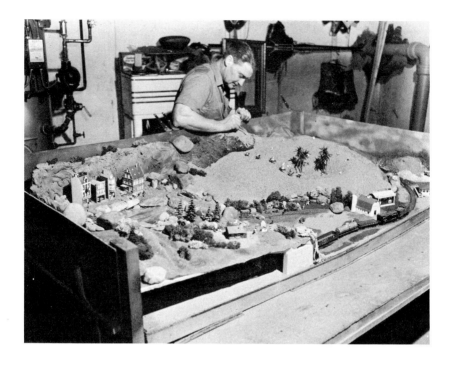

Fig. 5-1

It will seem to be a natural part of the whole scene when the entire layout is photographed. The division between background and foreground should never be obvious; they should seem to be continuous.

In Fig. 5-1, the relationship of the background and foreground are in scale with each other. The easiest way to achieve this is through the use of scale models and sets in miniature. I often use HO model railroad gauge as my size factor. This layout is in my own cellar and has proved quite convenient for personal — as well as professional — stills, movies, and videotaping. I often use this layout to prove that you can get excellent results even when working, where many must, amid the clutter of the average cellar, playroom, or garage. Actually, at home, I prefer the cellar since I can lock it and make this area off-limits to the children and curious adults when I have equipment out and layouts all ready to shoot.

We'll deal, initially, with two vital factors — lighting of sets with backgrounds and keeping the scale of these rear areas related to the foreground. In balancing the lighting, even such a precision light meter as the Weston Ranger 9 yields poor results. As with many types of craftsmanship in many fields, this is not any reflection on a fine tool. It would just be improper use of the tool. To the eye, the painting used as a background in Fig. 5-2a might look almost as well-illuminated as the foreground sand. To make balancing of light more simple, I have used brownish construction-type play-sand. This has been washed and treated for use as play-sand, but it is not as fine as white

Fig. 5-2a   Fig. 5-2b

sand. Technically, this sand is a little out-of-scale with the HO scale used for the figures, but since various sands do have different textures, this is not a vital point. However, the construction sand, though grayish, will reflect a great deal more light than the painted background. If we were to film according to a reading taken just of the painting, disregarding the sand, the sand area would wash out.

Figure 5-2b will give you an idea of the washed-out result obtained by meter readings of areas in the painting alone. As you can see, the painting reproduced nicely. This picture also illustrates why you should never use an out-of-scale figure. The horse and rider at the left of the painting are completely out of scale with the objects in the set and stand out like a sore thumb.

In Fig. 5-3a, the Weston Ranger 9 light meter is being used to read light values on the sand areas. Since this meter will read very small sections of the subject accurately, it is suitable for averaging results and balancing lighting. There are some tricks to the use of light meters, and they should definitely be applied when you use this type of meter.

For all readings, make sure the meter is aimed so that it will read the light that will be reflected directly into the camera lens.

Make sure that the meter is not casting a shadow on the area from which you are taking a reading.

Take a series of readings close to the background. Usually three will be enough: (1) a reading of lightest area, (2) a reading of darkest area, and (3) a reading of an area that is between lightest and darkest areas. Average these readings, and make a note of this average. Then take three readings with the meter held close to the different areas in the foreground, and average these readings. Make a note of this average. If your average light intensity on foreground and background are reasonably balanced, you are ready to make taking readings; that is, readings that you will translate into an exposure rather than, as was done, using them as indications of light intensity comparison. These final readings are taken at the camera, with the meter held so that it is in line with the lens, in order that the meter will read light reflected directly into the camera lens. Again, I suggest about three readings, each of different areas of background and foreground with an average, first, of each

Fig. 5-3a   Fig. 5-3b

set of three readings. Finally, an average of the readings of the background (from the camera position) and an average of the readings of the foreground (from the camera) should be added and divided by two in order to get a final average reading from the camera position. This average reading from the camera will usually give an excellent overall result if the foregoing procedure was followed.

By adjusting your lights in accordance with your very close light intensity readings, you should achieve an excellent balance in your lighting of both foreground and background. By double-checking readings taken directly from the subject with those taken from the camera position, your estimate of the best possible exposure should be on the nose. In time, you will find that you will be able to move your meter over a set, quickly noting variations and then quickly make one or two readings from the camera and come up with exactly the exposure you want. However, this only comes through experience. Even when you are an experienced professional, I suggest shooting not less than two takes, one at the calculated exposure and one deliberately underexposed one stop. This is especially important when shooting color. If underexposed, you will simply get a darker scene with deeper colors. If you overexpose a color scene, however, you will wash it out.

In Fig. 5-3b, the sand is lighter than the background, which is what we wanted. It is supposed to appear to be terrain not directly in back of the foreground scene, but as a desert in the middle-ground. By moving the camera in to photograph this area, we crop out the unrelated areas including the frame of the painting and the out-of-scale rider on horseback.

It is important to keep the lighting in background and foreground related, as in Fig. 5-4a. This flat, overhead lighting could not take place at any time except midday. It lacks the texture of either early morning or late afternoon sun, with hardly any shadows being cast.

Fig. 5-4b could have been taken in either early morning or late afternoon. Long shadows are being cast, and there is a great deal of texture to the sand and rock areas. The sun, however, would have to be at the cameraman's back, behind the camera.

When we combine a painted background with a desert foreground, as in Fig. 5-4c, we must have our lighting correspond to that in the painting. The

100

Fig. 5-4a   Fig. 5-4b

Fig. 5-4c

light in the painting is coming directly toward the camera. The light on our miniature set must seem to come from the same direction. In this scene I have deliberately set the light source about as far to the left of the setting sun in the painting as I dared. The light was set above and behind the painting. In setting your main light source, you have much more latitude in the vertical than in the horizontal. You will note that the shadows of the tree trunks are falling in a slightly incorrect line with the sun. This is what we mean by "horizontal" length misalignment. Shadow related to the elevation of the sun, is much more difficult for the audience to evaluate. Thus, if the shadows are long in a setting or rising sun, the audience will accept them as proper. The backlighting of the palms and their prominence in the scene will overshadow the less noticeable misalignment of the trees' shadows. Be most careful with your lighting. The more correctly it relates the background to the foreground, the better your chances are of achieving a fine, natural-looking result.

This is a perfect time to discuss another common error that occurs when the cameraman combines the real with the unreal. It is the problem of focus. There will be some tolerance of error because of the audience's tendency to overlook many details, especially during very short scenes. But you must not abuse this tolerance. The audience can apprehend a great deal in a split second, which is why very short scenes work.

Fig. 5-5a   Fig. 5-5b

Fig. 5-5c

Though the human eye does not see a whole area with crystal clarity, the mind is used to accepting distant scenes as being in-focus. The common error in focus related to shooting miniatures is caused by the cameraman who gets too close to the set with his camera. Because he is working with the camera focused only 14 to 20 inches, his depth of field is limited to only a few inches before and behind his actual point of focus. Both the foreground and back-drop in Fig. 5-5a are unnaturally out of focus. It is better to let the audience put things out of focus by that concentration on an important action. When the cameraman has already gone through the process for the audience, they will notice instantly that something is wrong.

In Fig. 5-5b, the cameraman has overcome his problem to an almost ac-ceptable degree. He has given his scene a longer exposure time (in a still camera), which allows him to use a much smaller aperture. This has increased his depth of field so that both the foreground and the painted background are almost in focus.

In Fig. 5-5c, the cameraman has employed an excellent solution; he has moved back a little so that he may now use the cabin as his actual point of focus. He knows that the cabin is the most central distance in this scene, being almost equidistant from the painting and the cliff in the foreground. He also knows that depth of field increases by about one-third to the fore and two-thirds to the rear of the actual point of focus. By moving back he has in-creased his depth of field. By focusing on a point a little deeper in the scene (the cabin instead of the bushes), he has increased the depth of field further. By using a fairly small aperture, he has provided himself with the final in-surance in regard to natural-looking sharpness.

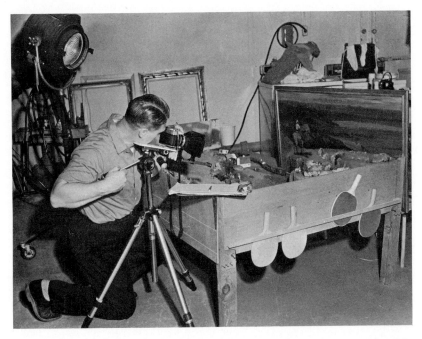

Fig. 5-6a

Obviously, if you are shooting still pictures or still slides, the above solution ends your problems. If, however, you are shooting a movie or videotape, I suggest slight animation of the figures, using this scene as the orienting long shot. Next I would suggest a rather close medium shot of the cabin and the figure at the door. Your third scene could show just the backdrop. From there on, there is no end of possibilities. For example, to create the illusion of the water moving, you could arrange a simple lighting effect to cast intermittent shadows, for a simulation of water movement. Moving a thin cloth with folds in it across a light source is one way of doing this. Another is to paint various shadings on acetate and move that across your light source. Yet another method with which you could experiment is using your movie projector to project a scene of moving water on the water area of the painting. In each of these instances, you will want to confine your water movements to the water area. Since the forest in the painting is so dark, it will not matter if the water effects overlap a little into the forest. You do want to be careful of the sky area, however, as the water effects would show up in these light areas. You may even wish to mask the light source or projector so your effects will definitely be limited to the water area of the painting.

In Fig. 5-6a, the 35mm Canon Pellix still camera is in place with the matte box being used as a light shade. A single klieg light (1000-watt bulb) is used as the source of illumination. With many scenes in which you employ a painted background, you can get by with a single source of illumination, even a home-movie 650-watt sun-gun or similar light. Of course, using reflectors and subdued fill-in lights will produce a superior scene.

103

In nature, the sky reflects a lot of light; so do bright clouds and very light surroundings such as sand and snow. This is especially true in the hours from about 10:30 A.M. to about 3 P.M. in the winter and even later in the summer. In early morning and late afternoon you will find the contrast between object shadow and adjacent front-lighted areas to be quite severe. You must learn to realize what you see in nature when you look at it. Study it, learn from it, and remember what you have learned, because many of your miniature scenes are intended to duplicate nature's lighting effects. For example, light on an overcast day is a lot bluer and brighter than you usually realize, and it will be diffused and flat all day. Light in the hours around sunrise and sunset is redder than that of the midday sun. Early morning and late afternoon sun creates harsher shadows and more contrast between directly illuminated surfaces and indirectly lighted areas.

I often prefer using my 35mm Canon Pellix still camera for making composite scenes in which there is no animation of objects. It gives me a greater depth of field because of choice of exposure times (from bulb to 1/1000 sec.) and a wide choice of apertures. Due to the variety of lenses it accepts, there is a wide choice of focal lengths, fields of vision, and depths of field. Furthermore, I can check the depth of focus directly through the lens at the f/stop I intend to use. I can also examine the lighting through the lens. There is a host of other advantages over the average movie camera.

After taking the 35mm still slide, I can later rephotograph it and reduce it to a color movie scene. A number of slides may be shot for considerably less money than an equivalent number of movie scenes. The best slide can then be chosen, and one movie scene, perfectly exposed, can be made of this slide, either by a laboratory or by you through projection. A small degree of animation may even be managed by taking a series of, say, 36 exposures in which each still picture represents a slightly more advanced stage of motion. This simply means using the roll of 35mm still film as though you were single-framing the action with a movie camera. If the scene runs longer than the 36 exposures, which it very well may, you can use more than one roll. Have the rolls developed as movie film would be, in a film strip, not divided into single frames. When the rolls of film are returned, splice them together in edited sequence. Then have the strip reduced to the size of movie film your projector will show (16mm, 8mm, or Super 8mm). By sending the film to a laboratory that is familiar with this type of work, it will cost you so little to have them splice the proper scenes together, I doubt that you would find it necessary or desirable to buy a 35mm splicer.

Now let us study the various ways in which the cameraman could have shot and exposed this composite of painted backdrop and miniature foreground. In Fig. 5-6b, he has produced a scene in which the background area almost competes with the foreground. In fact, the foreground area of the painting almost becomes a part of the foreground area of the set, and the upper, darker section of the painting appears to be the actual background of the lower two-thirds of the scene. This is not bad proportion: it is often acceptable to have a two-thirds foreground and one-third background or, conversely, a one-third foreground and two-thirds background. The proportion itself emphasizes the dominance of your main subject area. This is usually a contributing factor

104

Fig. 5-6b

Fig. 5-6c

Fig. 5-6d

in the accomplishment of superior composition. Unfortunately, in a case such as Fig. 5-6b, it requires a much more sophisticated blending of lighting between actual set and the foreground area in the painting. Melding the miniature terrain with the foreground of the painting means that you want to present both as being in the same plane. While the cameraman has eliminated the out-of-scale horse and rider at the left, he has not eliminated the out-of-scale brush at right. The unnatural areas of this scene will be too noticeable. An artificial appearance has crept in, and the effect of actuality has been destroyed.

In Fig. 5-6c, the cameraman has used three planes of interest. This is still acceptable from a compositional standpoint, because only one is truly dominant — the set foreground. This dominance is emphasized by proper exposure of the cliff and by a textured rendition through lighting of the entire set foreground. The light, as it is in all three of the examples, is well-aligned with the light and shadow of the painting. The foreground of the painting, the second plane, is considerably lighter than the background of the painting. The human eye will naturally move from the lighter set foreground to the darker foreground of the painting accepting this as another plane of vision. In making such a step, the audience allows the cameraman considerable latitude in exposure of set and backdrop without rejecting the composite scene as unnatural. The third plane in this scene is the dark background of the painting. The eye will move, very

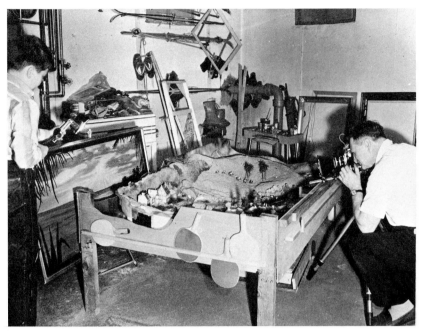

Fig. 5-7a

smoothly, to the background in the painting and will accept this as a third plane of vision. By introducing three planes, each at a different distance, the cameraman has given a comfortable, natural feeling of real depth to the scene. Consequently, the picture approaches an acceptable degree of reality, and the out-of-scale brush at the right is of considerably less consequence than in Fig. 5-6b.

Figure 5-6d shows the type of treatment you might use if you wanted to concentrate audience's attention on the set, preparatory to going in for some close shots of various details. In this picture the cameraman has moved the painting closer, eliminating not only the horse and rider at the left but also the out-of-scale brush at the right. By lowering the painting, he has eliminated its foreground entirely. While the darkness and shadings of the background of the painting are sufficient to create the illusion of various planes of vision, the cameraman has also tilted the painting slightly backward so the top is farther from the camera than the bottom. This slight backward tilt contributes further to the illusion of great distance and depth and yet is not sufficient to introduce distortion.

Another point in regard to your choice of backdrop: if you can use a scene such as this in which there is no animation in the backdrop itself, you will make your task a lot easier. Until you have become better acquainted with the techniques of animation, you will find you can often circumvent the problem of animation in the background by choosing one in which there is no real object movement or one in which object movement is extremely slight. Simplicity is often the keynote of success, especially in the early stages of your experiments with animation.

106

Fig. 5-7b   Fig. 5-7c

In Fig. 5-7a, the flexibility of our small group of sets becomes evident. By simply shooting from the other side of our multiple-set Ping-Pong table, we are able to shoot an entirely different type of set. The two scenes that follow were shot with a 650-watt, hand-held, home-movie-type light. If slower than 1/25 sec. is used, put the light on a stand so that the shadows do not move during exposure. Of course, if you are shooting with an ordinary movie camera, your exposure time will normally be faster than 1/25 sec. My son Richard has braced his arm here and is holding the light source very still. The painting is tilted slightly backward. An exposure close to movie-camera shutter speed was used. Again, I'm using my 35mm Canon Pellix and will rephotograph this picture later as a motion-picture scene, after I have selected the best slide. Two types of scene were shot: early morning and sunset. Three exposures were made of each scene.

In Fig. 5-7b you see a deliberate washing-out of the water in the foreground and of other highlight areas just as they might appear at that moment of intense brightness that takes place just after sunrise. The rooftops may still glisten with some early dew, and everything has a just-washed freshness, as the brightness of the day begins to break through full force.

In Fig. 5-7b, the tree leaves at upper left and upper right could be cropped out by moving the camera (or zoom lens) forward a little. I felt that the leaves added to the feeling of depth in the scene, so I left them in.

In Fig. 5-7c, we have a light effect similar to that in Fig. 5-7b, but with a darker background for simulation of the setting sun. In Figs. 5-7b and 5-7c, we have taken a great deal of poetic license with our lighting. If these scenes were to be used professionally, where technicalities would be important, one would have to move the light source to a position slightly above the backdrop behind the sun in the painting. The purpose in these two scenes, however, was to show up the small buildings in the little village. This is another illustration of latitude you can enjoy if you are careful not to abuse the audience's sense of reality. The trick is not to let the audience dwell on the scene. Leave it on the screen long enough for it to orient the audience and for it to be enjoyed, but not so long a time that the audience will start examining it.

There is no doubt that when you can get a backdrop of proper proportion and locale, you will find it considerably easier to utilize than a projected back-

107

ground. For one thing, it is far easier to get the proper lighting balance between set foreground and the painted backdrop than it is when working with either a front-projection or rear-projection setup. In projection, you are limited by the fall-off in intensity of light when the image has been projected quite a distance.

You have to be careful that you do not get glare or hot spots from your painted background. A shiny painting or a photograph on glossy stock will tend to glisten unnaturally and spoil your effect. You can remedy this in many ways. The angle of the light in relation to the camera and backdrop greatly affect glare. The horizontal and vertical angles of the painting can help control glare, as does diffused, soft lighting. Your backdrop may be coated with a dull, glare-resistant varnish, such as artists use to overcoat and protect their oils. Something like Matvar #53 varnish for oil or tempera paintings (made by F. Weber Co., Philadelphia, Pa.) will impart a dull matte finish to an objectionably shiny surface. The more coats you apply, the duller and less reflective the surface will become.

If you have a fine artist in your family or group or are doing a job commercially and can afford to hire one, you can make a very professional-looking backdrop. Just keep in mind that vanishing points, perspective lines, and scale relationships created in the background must relate to these in the foreground. The backdrop and set must appear as one scene.

Back-Projection: Still

Thus far we have dealt with backgrounds that are paintings or pictures of sufficient size to fill an adequate area behind a miniature set. These are opaque and are illuminated from the front, the side facing the camera. Often the same light source is used to light both backdrop and foreground subject matter. In the case of projected backgrounds, our next topic, illumination of the backdrop is entirely limited to that supplied by the bulb of the projector. This presents a problem. In some scenes, the background would naturally appear darker, in which case you have more latitude in your lighting. But whether or not your subject will allow no, some, or a lot, of margin between backdrop and foreground illumination, you are still going to have to concern yourself with the problem of softer, more diffused lighting than is used in shooting ordinary subjects or painted backdrops. An old friend of mine, Victor Solow of Solow Productions in New York City, suggested one of the most up-to-date solutions in providing soft light. It is a plastic material called Pio-Screen, which is made by the Piolite Plastics Corp., 210 Essex Ave., Gloucester, Mass. Pio-Screen is very resistant to flame and melting and can stand the heat of lights even if used a short distance from them. I like it better than any other type of material (ground glass, Fiberglas cloth) that I have used for the applications shown in this book. The roll I used to test the material for this book was 25 feet long, 49 inches wide, and 0.007 inches thick. To the touch, it feels about as thin as a heavy-piece of typing paper. It has a matte surface on both sides. This surface is not in the least shiny, yet it feels extremely smooth to the touch.

In a comparison test that I ran, with light, subject, and angle of light on the subject all identical, I found the following facts. Without any diffuser in front

108

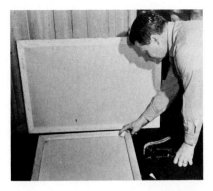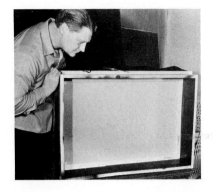

Fig. 5-8a   Fig. 5-8b

of the light source, the exposure had to be 1/30 sec. at $f/6.3$. With a ⅛-inch thick ground glass, the aperture had to be changed to $f/5.6$. With Pio-Screen plastic in place of the ground glass, the aperture had to be opened up to $f/3$ in order to get a good color scene. The ground glass required only one stop more, whereas the Pio-Screen required over three stops more exposure. The extra two stops were required because of the greater ability of the Pio-Screen to diffuse the light evenly. Because of its diffusing ability, Pio-Screen eliminates hot spots, even when a spotlight is used behind it. Naturally, if you do use any very strong light in which the rays are concentrated in a small area, as with a spot, try to keep a reasonable distance between the light and the plastic. Although Pio-Screen is rated as non-flammable and resistant to melting, you must use common sense and not expect the impossible.

As shown in Fig. 5-8a, Pio-Screen works well when stapled onto a wooden frame. Artist's wooden canvas-stretching frames are excellent and cheap. The corners of the wood are grooved, so that adjoining pieces fit into each other. The frame is assembled by fitting and pushing the corners together. A stapling gun can be used to staple the plastic to the face of the frame. The Pio-Screen should be cut a little smaller than the outer edge of the frame so it won't be torn, in use, by an overhanging piece of plastic getting caught on something. Put one staple every two inches so that the staples virtually stitch the Pio-Screen to the wood frame. Try to keep the plastic as tight as possible while you are doing this. (Be sure you work at a temperature around 70 degrees.) Once the plastic is stapled to the wooden frame, put the little wood chips in place in each corner, two to each corner. By driving these chips into spaces provided for them, you will spread the corners slightly. This is how the canvas is stretched tight when an artist mounts canvas on the frame. Do not overtighten the frame, or you may tear the plastic. Actually, when used as a diffuser, the plastic need not be very tight; it is only when the Pio-Screen is going to have images projected upon it that tightness is imperative. It is a good habit, however, to eliminate waviness from every screen you make.

In the beginning, you should make two frames measuring 24″ x 36″ and two measuring 24″ x 24″. This will provide you with one rear-projection screen (24″ x 36″), one large diffuser-reflector, and two smaller diffuser-reflectors.

109

Fig. 5-9

These should be ample for your initial exploration into diffusion and back-projection.

Figure 5-8b shows where your large rear-projection screen would be used. It is set up in a box made of shelving board, and painted black in its interior. The screen, on its wooden frame, fits into it and is held parallel to the rear of the box and perpendicular to its base.

In Fig. 5-9, the cameraman is using an Ampex Videotape camera to check special effects before filming the composite scene comprised of set and background projected onto the 24" x 24" screen held in the box discussed above. Four eye-screws have been screwed into the top and bottom of each of the three frames not used in the screens in the rear-projection box: two screws in the top and two in the bottom of each of the three frames. One diffuser is not being used in this scene and has been laid against the side of the miniature set table. The other 24" x 24" diffuser is held in exactly the right attitude by string running from the eye-screws in the top of the frame to the ceiling and from the bottom of the frame to the oak bench. This 24" x 24" diffuser is being used to diffuse and soften the light from a 650-watt movie-light, which is placed on a stand just beyond the bench at the right. Black cloth is laid around the projection box to help protect the rear-projected image on the screen from stray light rays. Note that the lights being used to expose this whole scene to show you how the screen, cameras, diffusers, and lights were arranged, are bright and not diffused. Also notice how this strong light, in the area not protected by the Pio-Screen diffuser, would wash out any image being projected on that

Fig. 5-10a   Fig. 5-10b

Fig. 5-10c   Fig. 5-10d

Fig. 5-10e

screen. Note, too, that the diffuser is angled slightly away from the background and is slanted a little downward. Thus, the light beams falling on the rear side of the diffuser are going to be directed away from the rear projection screen, but downward onto the set in the foreground. The idea is to lighten the shadow area of the set without weakening the rear-projected background image. For further diffusion, the Fiberglas in the large klieg light in the background of Fig. 5-9 has been replaced with Pio-Screen. You can see the completely even diffusion of light throughout this entire circle of light cast by the klieg light. The large 24″ x 36″ diffuser at the left serves as a reflector of stray light beams and will add very little to the scene. The movie camera, which will be later used to film some scenes of this set, is to the left just beyond the cameraman. The

111

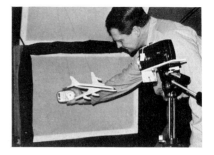

Fig. 5-11a   Fig. 5-11b

projector for the background scene is just to the right of the right side of the
rear of the projection screen box and to the left of lolly column about one-third
down from top of picture.

In Figs. 5-10a, 5-10b, 5-10c, and 5-10d, you will see how important it is to
balance foreground and background lighting and how easy it is to wash out a
projected background. In Fig. 5-10a, the cameraman balanced his light fairly
well, used his diffusers on the foreground well, but was careless about the light
spilling over onto the projection screen background. Thus, you will notice that
the background is weak in spite of the very dramatic cloud formation. Fig.
5-10b is acceptable, and the balance is good. In a full-color scene this lighting
would result in fine rendition of both foreground and background. In Fig.
5-10d, one undiffused spotlight was used, with the light directed, as shown in
Fig. 5-9, high and from the side, so that there would be little light bouncing
directly onto the background from the set. This yields a dramatic scene in
black-and-white, but the colors in a motion-picture scene or on a color slide
would be washed out in the foreground. Figure 5-10d shows how the Pio-Screen
diffusers soften the foreground light and perfectly balanced foreground and
background. An excellent black-and-white scene is obtained, but the results
would be just as good in color.

You wish the projected background to be exposed as much as possible, by
merit of its own light and none other. If other light falls on the background from
the front, it will weaken the image and will spoil color rendition of what is
supposed to be one natural scene.

In Fig. 5-10e, you see a scene in which, in nature, an element of bleakness
actually exists. The clouds creeping across the mountain tops thousands of feet
away, an overcast situation, and a brightness of light as it breaks through the
mist at a high elevation on our log cabin in foreground are as they appear in
nature. The whole key to lighting in this scene, both in the foreground and background, is uniformity. The scene has tremendous depth, even though its lighting
is quite flat, because the tones and gradations are real.

Figures 5-11a and 5-11b show two important steps in balancing the lighting
between foreground subject and projected background. The object here was to
show off a model airplane and to do it by having it seem in actual flight. Since
a background was to be rear-projected onto the 24″ x 34″ Pio-Screen set in the
projection box, the white model plane had to have almost the same illumination

Fig. 5-12a

Fig. 5-12b

Fig. 5-12c

as the background. First, I took a light reading directly off the projection screen with the scene projected onto it (not shown here). Then, holding the release button down on my Weston Ranger 9 meter, I ran the meter across and up and down the screen, noting the variations. If I wish to match a single color, as in this case, I take a reading of the white building in the background. Then I take a reading close to the plane, making sure I am not reading an area in the shadow of the meter or my hand. These two readings should vary little. If they do, I would have to increase or decrease the foreground lighting to the point where a reading of the white plane matches a reading of the white building. Scanning the projected background with the meter will still give one an idea of minimum and maximum range overall and will show up any hot spots, if they exist.

113

Figure 5-12a was lit only by light used to make the exposure of the actual composite picture in Fig. 5-12b. This time the 1000-watt klieg light was used, but the Fiberglas diffuser was replaced by a 24″ x 24″ Pio-Screen diffuser set up about 18 inches in front of the klieg light lens, tilted slightly downward and angled away from the process screen. The other two diffusers shown were used only as light reflectors and contribute very little to the illumination of the airplane. The Ampex Videotape camera is being used to check the effect. You will note on the TV monitor on the left that light spilling from behind the diffuser onto the TV screen washes out the scene. The same scene on the process screen is, however, even and not washed out. This is because care was taken to shield the screen from direct light. Black cloth all around the screen is stretched out along black support tapes that hold it away from the screen as far as possible without interfering with the lighting of the model plane. Even more important, only diffused light, whose beams have a very short range and will not reflect strongly from the plane into the background, is used to light the plane. Even this is directed, as much as possible, away from the background. Unless you can completely darken the room in which you are working, I suggest you do your rear-projections at night; otherwise daylight coming into the room will create all sorts of problems. Notice how completely dark it is around the subject and process screen when the whole area was photographed only by the light that would be used to expose the model plane and the projected background.

The projector used to project the background scene was the Bell & Howell 960 Slide Projector with a 500-watt lamp. This has an $f/3.5$ Bell & Howell Filmovara zoom lens. At a distance of about 12 feet from the rear of the projection screen, I have no trouble filling the 2′ x 3′ projection screen with a 35mm slide. For background projection, you should have a zoom projection lens capable of blowing up the image to the size of your screen within the confines of your space. You wish to avoid excessively long projection distances, because the light loss over long distances is bound to be great. You should also have a projector with a fine optical system: cheap projectors may create a hot spot in the center of your projected background. Your projector must be able to illuminate the entire scene evenly. As you can see, the projector used here does exactly that. The illumination is excellent overall, and it is even. The darker areas in the picture are areas that were actually darker on the projected slide.

Figure 5-12b shows the fine degree of matching that can be achieved between foreground subject matter and the background, even though the plane was stark white. The Pio-Screen diffusers can actually achieve tremendous screen and subject light balance.

On the other hand, you can arrange your diffusers and lights to create a scene that will feature the plane in its actual stark white without losing the background. This is shown in Fig. 5-12c. If your purpose was to show the plane, the White House, and its surrounding area in Washington with equal prominence, you would strive for an effect like that in Fig. 5-12b. If, however, you wished to feature the plane, you could soft-focus the background, light the plane strongly, and let the background go a little dark. In Fig. 5-12c, the background is a slightly out-of-focus backdrop to the model plane.

In Fig. 5-13a, other illumination was used in the room to give you a clearer idea of placement of the background scene projector. Naturally, this other illu-

114

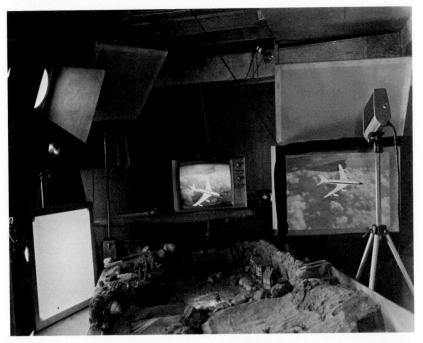

Fig. 5-13a

Fig. 5-13b

Fig. 5-13c

Fig. 5-13d

Fig. 5-13e

mination weakened the projected image on the process screen, but you can see it well enough to get an idea of how the scene was worked out. Again, the Ampex Videotape camera is on the right, and the TV monitor (set) is placed alongside the process screen box so the effect can be studied before the scene is shot. If you do not have videotape equipment, you can study the scene in the viewfinder of your camera, and can determine the balance of lighting with your light meter as discussed above. You can doublecheck this if your camera has a built-in light meter; but rely mainly on the hand-held meter. The built-in meter will probably read only one area of the whole scene, and that area might not include both the plane and the clouds.

For the scene in Fig. 5-13a, the klieg light contains the Pio-Screen diffuser. Its flaps (barndoors) are also set to shield the background screen but to allow full diffused illumination of the plane. A #1 photoflood in a reflector is set about one foot behind the 24″ x 24″ Pio-Screen diffuser in the lower lefthand corner. Both light sources are angled away from the background slightly, though they do point directly enough at the airplane to illuminate it completely. Even in the monitor screen, which has some direct external light spilling onto it from the #1 photoflood, you can see that the plane is excellently illuminated.

Figure 5-13b shows what a fine job of exposure balance has been achieved between the plane and the sky. In color this would make a most convincing scene. Actually the 35mm slide was taken from a jet, whose one motor and right wing may be seen in upper left. The model plane, seeming to pass below the wing of this jet, derives an extra degree of authenticity from the introduction of the real plane. Figure 5-13c shows a treatment in which the plane is made to appear whiter and the background darker. This shot emphasizes the model plane.

Figure 5-13d shows tremendous depth and careful matching of subject and background lighting. Figure 5-13e highlights the model plane. An illusion of great height is conveyed by the dark background. Here the background is secondary.

Back-Projection: Motion

Throughout this series, the model plane was hung stationary by black thread. If, however, you were going to make this a movie, you would have to pull the plane across the scene. One hole would be bored entirely through the outboard motors on the right and left sides of the plane. Another hole would be bored through the nose of the plane, and still another through the tail. One thread would pass through the motor on the right, and the right side of the plane would be supported by this thread. Another thread would pass through the motor on the left side to support the left side. A third thread would pass through the body of the plane. These three threads would allow you to support the plane in almost any attitude, especially if the plane were to move across the background at only one level. A fourth thread would be attached to the nose of the plane on the side away from the camera, so that the plane could be pulled along the support threads during shooting. If the threads showed up in the scene, they could be

116

painted to match the background. With fine nylon fishline and soft, diffused light, however, you might get away without touching up the thread.

Movement can be imparted to a completely stationary subject, such as this plane, turning the camera slowly across the subject in a well-controlled pan. As you pan, simulating subject progress, you might also zoom in toward the subject. Thus, to hide your subterfuge, you would really simulate two subject movements — movement across and up toward the camera. This can be most effective, but is a technique involving some practice, testing, and prudent selection of subject matter, background, and camera angle. For example, a model plane such as this is ideal, because there are no turning wheels to contend with.

Another way to simulate forward progress, which is commonly used in professional movies, involves the use of a projection screen, usually the rear-projection type described above. A motion picture scene, with proper action, is projected in back of the subject (*e.g.*, a driver of a car). I suggest that you experiment with this type of moving background, as it opens vast areas of trick and effect photography to you. I have had excellent results in making scenes needed for projection with my Bell & Howell Focustronic Super 8mm movie camera. I then projected these scenes onto the process screen set in the rear-projection box. As they were being projected, I photographed the subject. I made no attempt to synchronize projector or camera motors, and I have gotten away with it to date. I'm sure you too can be as lucky. If you are not, you can always revert to working with slide-projected still scenes and still glean a great deal of benefit from the technique of rear-projected backgrounds.

You should know, of course, why you may run into the problem of synchronization, even if you don't. The reason is this: motion pictures are nothing more than a series of still pictures. These are made by the camera exposing a series of still pictures. To do this the movie camera has a shutter that opens and closes many times during the making of a single scene. Each time this shutter opens, the film is held firmly in place, so that the image will not be blurred. While it is held still, one frame is exposed. As soon as that picture is made, the camera mechanism transports the film to the next frame, so that the next picture in the movie scene may be made. And herein lies our problem. During that flash of time, in which the film is transported, the camera's shutter closes and blocks out the light. This happens so quickly that you never stop to think about it. When your projector projects the movie scene onto the screen, it, too, has a shutter, and it, too, must close while the film is transported. Thus, when you are filming a film, you run the risk of having one shutter closed while the other is open. When this happens, no image will be recorded, and we say the movie camera and projector are "out of sync." There is equipment which can synchronize the camera with the projector, but it is costly. If you need it, I would suggest looking into the possibility of renting such equipment before you actually purchase it, so that you know exactly what will best suit your needs prior to making any sizeable investment. Meanwhile, take a chance with your equipment. The camera and projector might happen to sync. well enough so that, for the few scenes in which you'd actually need to use this technique, you can get by simply projecting movie scenes onto your background.

I have even had great luck running my projector backwards and refilming a scene for which I wanted reverse action. Also, I've been fortunate in filming scenes shot onto adjoining mirrors creating disappearing images as the subjects walk toward the area in which, for instance, two mirrors adjoin. How do you fit all these things into a book, let alone a chapter? I can only point the way.

Front-Projection

I have not taken the time to go into front-projection of backgrounds for lack of space and because I have found no need to use this technique, but I will discuss it briefly in case you wish to explore it. Instead of projecting the background onto a translucent surface, you project onto a screen akin to the ordinary movie screen onto which you normally project your slides and movies. I suggest you experiment with a regular movie screen before investing in any special equipment. Any screen having a high reflectance factor will do. In this type of photography the cameraman depends upon the foreground subject being strong enough so the background (projected onto both background and subject) will not show on the foreground subject. The subject is placed and the camera is set, usually head-on, so any shadow from the subject will fall in back of the subject and will not be recorded by the camera.

In front-projected background technique, a beam-combiner is often used. A two-way mirror can be used as a beam-combiner. Once you get into using these, however, you will run into other problems. If you wish to explore the matter further, I suggest going to your local library and browsing through books that delve into this particular field. Also, contact firms selling or renting equipment for front-projected backgrounds and discussing with them the techniques currently employed by professionals. Meanwhile, you can experiment with the projection screen you now own, especially if it is a good glass-beaded one.

One technique is to project the image directly onto the screen in back of your subject without worrying about part of the scene being projected all over your subject. Make some test exposures on movie film, and see what your results are. You may often be happily surprised.

Another method is to project the background at an angle — trying not to make it so acute that distortion occurs — so that it misses the subject.

118

6

Animation

The mysteriously sudden appearance or disappearance of objects and people — as if from (and to) nowhere — can be accomplished easily in motion pictures and videotaping. Any kid can dream of a Genii, and through the magic of special effect photography, those dreams can come true. Inanimate objects can be made to move. Toys and models can be manipulated to possess fascinating, lifelike motion. There is no end to possibilities.

One of the most pleasant and enjoyable aspects of animation is the ease with which some of it can be accomplished. Suppose you were shooting a sequence of motion-picture scenes about a child playing with a group of small toys. It would certainly add to the human interest if the child's small puppy dog were to appear magically in the midst of these stuffed animals, as if one of them had mysteriously come alive.

Performing the Supernatural

The magical appearance of the puppy dog amid the toys is a highly effective special effect. While it is apparently accomplished by your connivance with the supernatural, the very ease with which it is done is the most amazing feature of the whole trick. For instance, first shoot a scene of the child playing with the toys, then one of him standing and making some mysterious passes over the plastic animals. Next, you need a close shot of the toys alone. Once this close-up has been shot (such as the scene in Fig. 6-1a, Scene 6-1a), you must take care that the camera is not moved and that everything within the scene remains in exactly the same position between shots. The following scene must be made immediately. Carefully put the puppy dog into the central area of the picture, trying to hold his attention so that he will remain there until the camera has started. You wish to make a scene similar to Fig. 6-1b. Once the camera is rolling, anything that moves, including the puppy, is OK. The trick is to have everything exactly the same at the end of Scene 6-1a and at the beginning of Scene 6-1b, except for the inclusion of the puppy at the start of Scene 6-1b. Now, when Scene 6-1a is projected, it will immediately be followed by Scene 6-1b. Since the only difference between the end of Scene 6-1a and the beginning of Scene 6-1b is the inclusion of the puppy, the little dog will mysteriously pop onto the

119

Fig. 6-1a   Fig. 6-1b

screen amid the toys as if by pure magic of the highest order. To the audience Scenes 6-1a and 6-1b are *not* two scenes. They appear as *one* continuous scene.

Objects, people, almost anything, can be made to appear in this fashion. If you wish to make anything disappear, you just reverse the procedure. To make the puppy disappear, for example, shoot Scene 6-1b first, and at its end carefully remove the dog. Then shoot Scene 6-1a without the dog in the picture, and the puppy will disappear as magically as he appeared. The secret is the inclusion, or removal, of the subject of your occult powers between scenes, while the camera is not running, without changing the position, lighting, camera angle, or anything else about the rest of the scene between camera stop and camera start. The change must be made between the shooting of two immediately adjacent scenes.

With your new-found powers, it is no problem to get yourself a smoke the easy way. A forefinger, endowed with supernatural power, opens the cigarette box and causes the cigarette to float up between the fingers. What about a light? Your new-found invisible associates provide you with a candle at the wave of your hand; another flick of that all-powerful right hand of yours, and the candle lights up. Who needs old-fashioned lighters, anyhow? To the viewer, these happenings will be most mysterious, but to you, again, the accomplishment involves neither selling your soul to the devil nor any kind of occult aid.

To the audience, Figs. 6-2a, 6-2b, 6-2c, and 6-2d would all be part of the same scene in which the camera had never stopped. Actually, they are four separate scenes. But between scenes, nothing except the "animated" objects can be moved; the camera must remain absolutely stationary and set for the same distance, etc. Here is a short scenario for these scenes:

Figure 6-2a, Scene 6-2a: At end of scene, subject points finger at cigarette box, moving finger slightly back and forth, then making slight upward motion with forefinger. Stop camera.

NOTE: We are counting Scene 6-2b as *one* scene but it has *two* segments.

Scene 6-2b: Before starting camera, open cigarette box. Take out a cigarette. Wrap a thin black thread around half a toothpick; wrap it tightly so it will not slide off. Push the toothpick into the end of the cigarette until it no longer shows. Run thread between two fingers that will hold cigarette. Start scene with mouth-end of cigarette resting just on top of (now open) cigarette box. Subject should be posed exactly as shown in the first scene. When camera starts, subject's right hand (holding the thread unseen by the viewer) moves up to his

120

Fig. 6-2a

Fig. 6-2b

Fig. 6-2c

Fig. 6-2d

chin. Thread will be pulled through fingers of left hand lifting cigarette up and out of box. As far end of cigarette reaches edge of open box, stop camera. Cigarette almost clear of box, has just a short way to go to come to rest in left hand. Remove thread from cigarette and place cigarette between fingers of subject, who has not moved. Start camera. Run off a little film while subject makes mysterious motions with right hand. Stop camera. Don't let subject move.

Scene 6-2c: Place candle alongside cigarette box, while subject holds pose. Start camera and have subject make a few more passes with right hand. Stop camera, having subject hold pose.

Scene 6-2d: Light candle. Start camera and have subject continue with natural action, lighting cigarette from candle flame.

When you project this film, here is what will take place before the audience's eyes: The subject will make some magical motions at the cigarette box. It will pop open at his command and, seemingly imbued with some mystical power, a cigarette will lift itself up and rise over the edge of the box from which point it will seem to pop over right between the subject's fingers. A few more gestures and a candle appears out of nowhere; some more passes and the wick bursts into flame. The audience will assume that the camera never stopped and that they are seeing continuous, uninterrupted action. The whole illusion is really most effective, the results exceptionally gratifying. Just be careful that only those things that you wish to have move between scenes are the only things that are moved. Otherwise you will destroy the illusion. Take pains with the stopping and starting sections as well as with the changing of things between scenes, and your results can be most professional. If you wish to heighten the effect, you can

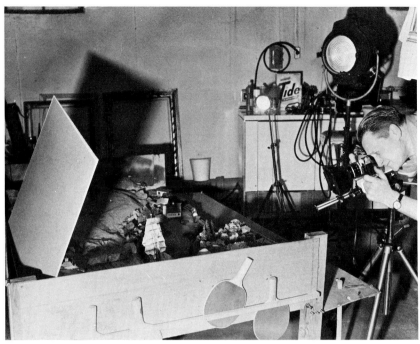

Fig. 6-3

always inject some puffs of smoke, etc., but first shoot this type of effect without embellishment, as simply as possible. Once you have the technique down pat, you have ample time later to improvise, improve, and add extra window dressing in future shooting.

Animation in Sets

In Fig. 6-3, a model boat is being photographed in a miniature set. A white canvasboard stands behind the sailing boat, out of view of the camera; it is used to soften some of the shadows. You could, of course, shoot the following animation with any movie camera having a single-frame control; this would be the easiest way of doing it. If, however, your equipment does not have a single-frame device, you can always take a series of still pictures, as is being done here, and have these incorporated into your movie film by a lab. You have to make sure, of course, that you shoot enough frames to fill a sufficient length of movie film to make a decent length scene. (We'll go into this in more detail a little later on.) For the sailboat scene, I used a 35mm camera, but only because it provides prints easily reproducible for this book. My Bell & Howell motion-picture camera has a single-frame device so I would normally shoot animated motion pictures directly on movie film.

In Fig. 6-4a, you see what can be a very common error in shooting animation in miniature sets — a very out-of-focus foreground. This is usually due to lack of consideration of depth-of-focus when shooting so close. In this scene,

122

Fig. 6-4a   Fig. 6-4b

the cameraman focused on the small rowboat just beyond the sailing craft. The point of focus was correct because depth of field extends less into the foreground and more into the background. The photographer simply forgot to work at a small enough aperture to insure sufficient spread in the depth of field; the result is very unnatural. What you must keep in mind in shooting miniatures is that in order to get the foreground, sailing craft, and the small village all into the same picture in real life, you would have to be quite a distance away and your camera would be set at greater than 50 feet, no doubt focused on infinity. At such a real distance, the foreground would, of course, be sharp. When you are working in miniature, however, your camera is going to be focused at close-up distances. The closer you focus, the less the depth of field.

This shot was made at $f/2.8$. Thus, not only was the lens focused at a close distance, but it was at a very large opening. Close focus plus a large lens opening combine to give the least possible depth of field.

In Fig. 6-4b the lens was stopped down to $f/8$ — and it remained focused on the rowboat. Without changing the point of focus, but closing down to a relatively small lens opening, I could carry the focus all the way from the immediate foreground, through the area in which the boats are, and back through the area in which the village stands. The very slight softening of the most immediate foreground is not only desirable; it better simulates the vision of the human eye. Let's not forget that while the eye has a tremendous field of vision — about 140 degrees horizontally and 110 degrees vertically — it only focuses sharply on the narrow segment of this vast area. The eye sees sharply the major area of interest and is only aware of most of the other things in its field of vision. Thus, the appearance of the scene in Fig. 6-4b is fine.

You can often combine techniques and special effects to create even more realistic results. In Fig. 6-5a, you see why we were hiding the lower section of the picture with the foreground. The sailing craft is really quite large in relation to the village, and it is on a stand that would be difficult to conceal. By using the binocular cut-out in a matte box, we can create the illusion of a craft sailing past the village when it would not have room to do so if we were to show the whole area. We will not show all the necessary frames to create an illusion of smooth motion as this example is being used just to give you the general idea of how to animate such a scene. In order to make the ship sail out of view of the binoculars, you move it slightly between each single frame you shoot. Nothing else moves between frames except that which you may want to seem to be mov-

Fig. 6-5a

Fig. 6-5b

Fig. 6-5c

Fig. 6-5d

ing; that is, the figures on the boat and on land may move slightly and the sails may be moved a bit to very slightly different angles to simulate movement by the wind. The important thing is to move the ship very little and with an almost imperceptible roll forward between each frame (Figs. 6-5b, 6-5c, 6-5d).

Before I go further in the area of animation, it is necessary to review briefly what single-framing is, as it is vital to animation. Most motion-picture cameras are equipped with a single-frame control. The Bell & Howell that I have has a threaded hole in the starting button. To single-frame, you simply screw a cable release, such as is used on still cameras, into this threaded hole. When you depress the cable-release plunger and release it immediately, the camera will expose just one frame on the Super 8mm movie film. Other cameras, which have no such arrangement, can still be used but it takes a little practice to be able to do it properly. Normally, if a camera does not have a cable-release arrangement, by quickly and crisply pressing and releasing the starting button, you can expose one frame only. If you delay, just a little, more than one frame will be exposed and all is lost.

The reason why single-framing is so important in animation work, in which a whole series of stops and starts are involved, is that if you were merely to stop and start your camera normally, the first few frames would usually be overexposed. The reason is that it takes many camera motors a split second to drive the film through the camera on speed. The inertia of the mechanism must be overcome in the starting. It takes a few frames for this to happen. If you take some of your film and hold it up to the light, you will notice that at the beginning of each new scene there are one or two frames at the head of the scene that appear lighter than the balance of the scene. Once the camera gets up speed, it exposes the rest of the film evenly, but those first few frames are over-exposed because the shutter turns over more slowly and stays open a little longer.

Not all cameras do this. It is a far more common problem in wind-up, spring-driven cameras than in electric-motor-drive ones. For example, my Bell & Howell Focustronic Super 8mm camera is battery-driven, and it does not seem to have any problem in overcoming inertia instantly. (If anything, there is a very slight underexposure in the first frame, and this is so slight that I doubt that it ever would be noticed in projection.) I would say that if you are going to do anima-tion work with any electric-drive camera, it is important to use batteries that are fresh and that operate at full voltage for their entire life. It is my opinion that if the electric motor in your camera is a good one, if your camera is peri-odically serviced so that its peak operation is maintained, and if the motor is receiving full voltage, the resultant surge of impulse to the motor at the start of the camera would overcome the inertia of the mechanism and give you a normal exposure in all frames including the first ones. At the worst, the surge of power with the first touch of the starting button might whip the shutter around just a little faster than normal, but the result should be almost imperceptible.

This difference between types of cameras and various makes is why, when you get into the business of single-framing and animation, you must make tests with your particular equipment. Even if your camera is designed for single-framing there might be a slight difference in exposure time between the single-frame exposure at a given film speed and the exposure of each frame when the camera is set at the same film speed but is running the film through an entire scene without stopping. Where such variance does exist, it is quite common for equipment that exposes at normal film speed of 1/30 sec. to expose at 1/20 or 1/25 sec. when single-framing. In order to determine if such variances exist, you must include in the test scenes an easily read description of the film speed, the f/stop, estimated exposure, and any other pertinent information you can think of. A vague test is no test at all. Once you know exactly what your camera does, then you will know what you are doing. Until you are sure of the performance of your equipment, you are operating in a state of limbo and confusion.

If you are single-framing with either a movie or a still camera (the 35mm to be reduced later to your film size), and you wish to know how many frames you'll need, first determine the number of seconds you want the scene to run on the screen. Once you decide how long the scene is to remain on the screen, all you have to do is multiply the number of seconds it is to be viewed by the number of frames per second you are shooting. The product will be the number of individual frames that will be required. For example, suppose you wished a motion-picture scene to be on the projection screen for two seconds. If you were using my Bell & Howell Super 8mm camera at normal speed, you'd be running about 18 frames per second. Thus, if you wished a two-second scene, you would use the following equation:

$$2 \text{ (seconds)} \times 18 \text{ (frames per second)} = 36 \text{ (frames)}$$

This will also give you a clue as to how to create smooth-running action. Smooth action is created by equal parts of action. In other words, the action

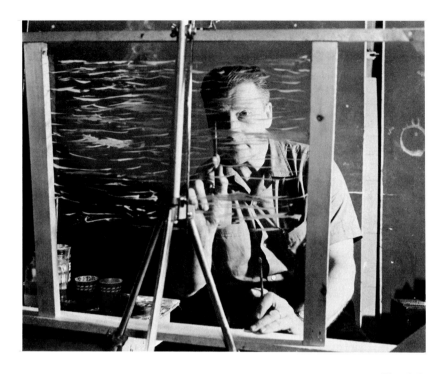

Fig. 6-6a

would be divided into equal segments throughout your scene. A simple explanation would be that if you wished to move a toy car over 36 inches of space in the scene, in a two-second long, 36-frame scene, you would move the car one inch between each frame. This would give you a total of 36 equal moves, advancing the car exactly the same distance between each exposure. If you wished jumpy action, you would move the car unequal distances between each exposure. We will get into the relation of movement to simulated speed and action in more detail later. There is, of course, more to it than I have just indicated.

One of the most useful properties in the world of animation is the *cell*. A cell is usually made of clear acetate and is normally of medium or heavy weight so that it is flexible but will not wrinkle easily. The cell is usually discussed in reference to animating cartoons. I'd like to introduce you to a more fundamental use that the average cameraman might use often. One use is to make artificial water in a miniature set look more realistic without using actual water. While a mirror is fine for a still lake, it is too still for most bays or any type of sea. If you look at any fine oil paintings of water scenes, you will see that the artist usually creates the illusion of moving water by applying shades of colors in many wavelike strokes. By introducing shadings the water appears to move. In Fig. 6-6a, I am painting various shades of wave strokes on a piece of clear acetate, a cell. The cell was simply thumb-tacked into place on one of the frames used for my oil paintings. The waves that are nearest the spectator are a little further apart and the waves that are further from the spectator are spaced a

Fig. 6-6b   Fig. 6-6c

little closer together. In making cells of this type you must remember to relate to realism. Think of how, if you really were the supposed distance from the subject, it might be seen. You must also keep in mind the resultant effect in relation to the surroundings, and keep everything related in perspective and proportion.

In Fig. 6-6b, you can see that the completed cell has been cut to fit the contour of the area into which it will fit. The fit should be tight and snug. It is wise to make a paper cut-out first so that if you make a mistake, you will not ruin your cell. When the paper cut-out fits perfectly, lay it on top of the cell, and using the paper as a template, cut out the cell.

In Fig. 6-6c, the cell is in place, and the scene, representing early morning or late afternoon, becomes very realistic. The illusion of realism may be further enhanced by single-framing. Between each frame, move the cell, the little boat, and some of the background figures, ever so slightly, so that the motion of both the water and some of the objects within the scene will contribute further to the simulation of real-life action. By using a cell that will not wrinkle but will bend easily, you can even create slight swells, small crests, and troughs in the waves. You could also employ more than one cell, spacing the waves a little further apart on one than the other. Move one beneath the other between single frames so that the actual lines of the waves on each different cell would move in projection. You must, of course, take care that you do not allow unnatural gaps to appear near the shore, and that the simulated action closely resembles the natural action you are attempting to imitate. Figuring out such challenging problems and coming up with the best possible result is one of the most satisfying rewards of doing animation.

Incidentally, note that the lighting has a definite purpose in relation to our binocular scene. Remember we said we were attempting to have the sailing vessel sail out of the right side of the scene when there really wasn't room. It would be natural for scenes of the village to follow the scene in which the sailing vessel had been watched through binoculars. By the lighting in Fig. 6-6c, we create, in addition, the illusion that the bay opens to the sea to the left of the scene, which is in deep shadow. The audience, therefore, accepts that the vessel had sailed off to the left even if this scene immediately followed the binocular scene.

Also note that the clarity of the foreground, while not needle-sharp, is most

127

natural. It is virtually how the human eye would perceive the foreground when viewing the village and the small boat. If you do not think this is so, place something that is needle-sharp (*e.g.*, some printed words) over the foreground, and look at the rowboat or the village. You will find that while you will be aware that the printed matter is there, it will not be clear enough to read. This realism in focus is simple to achieve with through-the-lens viewing, especially if you have a way of checking depth of focus.

As I have warned before, and will repeatedly warn again, do not let an effect, or trick, blank out your mind to the rest of what you ought to be aware of. Always coordinate everything with the special effect. The question is not of trick *or* treat, but of trick *and* treat. The trick should simply contribute to the overall perfection of your photographic effort. But it should never steal the show.

Animation can be most complex and expensive. The most professional employment of it requires the services of top-rank artists and animation experts. Animation of the type used in professional cartoons, which involves many movements of figures, objects, and setting within the scene can require as many as 24, or more, different single frames for each second of viewing. You can realize, therefore, that in order to make a one-minute commercial, you might need as many as 60×24, or 1440 different drawings in order to come up with enough frames, to show normal action in usual TV or professional motion-picture projection. (Sound-on-film motion pictures are projected at the rate of 24 frames per second. TV picture formation runs about the same speed for normal action.) This gives you a new appreciation of the vast undertaking involved in making something like a full-length motion-picture cartoon.

This book does not pretend to prepare you to make an epic like *Snow White and the Seven Dwarfs*. However, there is much that can be done by any careful and interested photographer in the field of animation. Normally, the procedure in doing a cartoon-style animation is to draw the background of the scene on paper, then draw sections that are required to move on transparent cells, which are laid one on top of the other. Both the background and the cells have exactly aligned holes punched in them so that they will fit one on top of the other in perfect register. The holes fit over pins in the registration boards. A complicated cartoon involving several different movements taking place at the same time in each frame would require several cells, laid one on top of the other over the still background. After each separate frame has been exposed, the cells are removed and a new set of cells with the new phase of movement is placed over the background, again in perfect register with the background and with the preceding set of cells. Only the areas in which movement has occurred are slightly out of register, and the change of register is only in those areas that are supposed to be moving, which creates the illusion of movement.

Cartoon-type animation is a whole field in itself, and if you are interested in it I suggest you go to your local library and check into some of the professional books on the subject. You might also write various book publishers, especially those concerned mainly with photography, such as Amphoto, 915 Broadway, New York, N. Y. 10010, and inquire as to other books that might deal with this phase of animation in greater detail.

In this book I'm more concerned with your being able to do special effects with animation and to help you breathe a special bit of realism into otherwise unreal objects such as toys, model railroads, and the like. This type of animation is most useful in educational, business, and various hobby fields. Further, it is not difficult to do.

The most common problem you will have to face in attempting to animate objects in a miniature set is the problem of scale. There are certain acceptable behavior patterns related to auto speeds, explosions, human movement, and almost every imaginable type of action. To maintain the audience's credulity, you must be careful to maintain certain standards. A common illustration of this problem is the car going off the cliff. If the cliff and the car are built to the scale of $1'' = 1'$, the scale is 1 to 12. A 12-foot car would, in this miniature, be 1 foot long, and a cliff 120 feet high would be 10 feet high in the miniature. Although everything else is in proportion, the rate of descent of the miniature car, if allowed to fall freely, would not be. The miniature would fall through space as fast as a 4000-pound car and would reach the bottom of the 10-foot cliff in about 4/5 sec. A real car would take about three seconds to fall 120 real feet off a real cliff, if some time were allowed for the fact that it would not fall straight down but, at high speed, would travel in a rapidly diminishing arc off the cliff, moving almost horizontally due to momentum for a very short distance.

One way of compensating for a free-falling miniature is to speed up the motion-picture camera, using slow motion (more frames per second) to adjust to the number of exposures that would normally be made of the falling object in real life, per each second of the fall. There is a mathematical formula that you may use to equate real and miniature falling object rates, and to determine how many frames would be needed to simulate the action involved. Where gravity is involved, as in explosions, falling objects, and lapping waves (without any other artificial impetus being applied), the miniature scale action is equal to the square of the time scale. The formula to employ is:

$$\sqrt{\frac{D \text{ (distance of real object)}}{d \text{ (distance of miniature)}}} = \text{(factor for camera-speed increase)}$$

In the example of the plunging car which was a one-twelfth scale model of the real car, the real 12-foot car would plunge off a real 120-foot cliff. The 1-foot miniature car would plunge off a 10-foot cliff. Thus, D would be 120 feet and d would be 10 feet. Inserting these figures in our formula, we must find the square root of 120/10, or the square root of 12. Since the square root of 12 is 3.5, we have a factor of 3.5. If we were using a Super 8mm camera, which exposes normal speed at about 18 frames per second, we would multiply 18 by 3.5 getting a product of 63 frames each second. If we were shooting at a professional speed of 24 frames per second, we would multiply 24 by a factor of 3.5 thereby getting a product of 84 frames per second. Obviously, as you work with smaller and smaller scale, your camera speed would have to be jacked up higher and higher. As you can see, utilizing fast camera speed to compensate for miniaturization would hardly be practical for the average movie fan as many, many cameras have a limit of 36 frames per second for slow motion. This would mean you would have to work with a one-quarter scale. With a 1-to-4 scale, you would have to build a cliff 30 feet high to simulate a 120-foot cliff, and the car would have to be 3 feet long. This, of course, is not very practical either. It seems still less practical to try to speed up the motion-picture camera when you realize that many of you will be working with an HO railroad scale, or something slightly larger or smaller. HO railroad scale is about 1 to 86, so you would probably have to work with camera speeds of over 200 frames per second. Since many professional cameras cannot go over 64 frames per second, you must find another way to simulate gravity fall. First, however, for your convenience I have included a table of the standard model-railroad scales:

Gauge	Scale	Measurement
O	1:48	¼" to 1'
S	1:64	3/16" to 1'
OO	1:75	4mm to 1'
HO	1:86	3.5mm to 1'
TT	1:120	1/10" to 1'

To return to our example of the 120-foot cliff: A solution does suggest itself when we realize that it would take a real car about three seconds to fall a real 120 feet. If we were working in HO gauge (1:86 scale), the 12-foot car would be reduced to 12 × 3.5mm = 42mm or about 1⅝ inch long. (There are approximately 25mm to each inch.) The cliff would be 120 × 3.5mm = 420mm (approximately 17 inches) high. To slow the falling action to a natural pace, we would have to take approximately 220 frames of the car in its descent. Since the car is 42mm long and must fall 420mm in about three seconds, it must fall about 140mm each second the scene is on the screen. If normal speed is 18 frames per second, then the 140mm must be divided into 18 equal distances of fall. Thus, in each frame, the car would be about 8mm closer to the ground. I think, by now, you may have guessed the solution. Between each single frame, you *artificially lower* the car a total of 8mm. Since you will be running your projector at about 18 frames per second and the entire scene will be on screen a total of three seconds, you know that your projector will show 54 frames in three seconds. Fifty-four times 8mm makes a total of 432mm of fall shown in 54 single frames. This slight difference will not matter materially. In fact, it will contribute to making the effect even more realistic.

Actually you should go one step further, as a real car going over a real cliff will not fall at exactly the same speed through the whole fall. When it first zooms off the cliff, the car will travel almost straight out. Once the rear of the car is half a car length out from the cliff, the heaviest part of the car (in most cars this would be the front) will begin to arc abruptly downward. Thus, you'd have to utilize from three to six frames just to get the car off the edge of the cliff and starting its full nose-dive. The downward plunge would be less rapid at the top than at the bottom, because the car would gain velocity the further it fell. Consequently, when the car leaves the cliff, it should travel first forward a little, then arc lazily downward, travelling less than a full 8mm each frame. To slow up action you move the object a shorter distance between each frame. As the car falls downward, you want it to fall further and further between each frame. To speed up action you move the object a greater distance between each frame. Thus, about midway down the plunge the car will be falling in

130

8mm drops between each frame, but from that point on it should fall a little further than 8mm between each frame. This would properly show a natural acceleration of free fall in real life. Don't expect your first results to be perfect. Perfection in this field is a combination of mathematical formulation, precision movement between frames, and quite a bit of flying by the seat of your pants. So until you have some experience with which to temper the calculations, the films you make of this type are apt to be somewhat unnatural. Don't be disappointed. Take careful note of just what you did so that you will know exactly how to experiment with adjustments.

How do you get the car to fall the proper distance between each single frame of exposure? Use either very fine transparent fishline or fine black thread. Hang the car from a couple of lines (in such a way that their attachment does not show). You can now cause it to fall as you wish, possibly even having it twist and turn a little in descent if you feel that would yield a more natural effect. Do not lower the car in a dead plumb line; in real life it would not fall that way.

In this type of animation another problem presents itself. Toys or models hardly ever break up under impact (unless they are specially prepared to do so) the way real objects do. One reason is that the impact is not as great, by any stretch of the imagination. Another reason is that the metal (plastic or wood) is relatively far thicker than would be the metal on the real thing. You can go to great lengths to weaken the model or drop it accurately on the right spot from a greater height than indicated by scale and attempt to start your camera a split second before impact, catching the break-up in slow motion. However, this is complicated and difficult. I suggest the subterfuge. One effective trick would be to have the camera move in close for the moment of impact, when the car is immediately engulfed in smoke and flame and the gas tank explodes. Small air-hose nozzles, set just below the surface of the ground and covered with plaster of Paris, could be covered with scale earth and rock. A blast of air at moment of impact would blow the earth, rocks, and white smoke of the plaster of Paris into the air, creating an excellent obliteration of the scene.

If you wish to introduce fire, be certain there is a fire extinguisher handy and that you know what you are doing. With combustible mixtures, experiment first in a very safe area outdoors. I suggest a mixture of a small amount of gasoline with a large quantity of kerosene. The gasoline produces a quick flash and the kerosene adheres to the surfaces of the models and burns more slowly with a flame that will register well. Since you are single-framing, you could introduce the flame explosion between any adjacent frames you'd deem best. The explosion of flame and consequent burning hides the actual break-up of the model. For the explosion you could move the camera back. Again, I must warn you about working with highly inflammable materials. Have only the small amount necessary for your effect on hand; keep large containers in another area. Use the mixtures sparingly, just enough to get the job done. (Not all fire extinguishers will work on everything; be sure the one you have is right for the mixture you are using.) Also have an ample water supply available in case other objects are affected. Have extra help around to aid in any extinguishing that may be necessary. Have a container that you can invert over the fire to smother it when you wish it to go out; this also produces photographically effective smoking of the ruins. When the fire is stopped, before you show what

131

is left, you can further demolish the model to coincide better with what would have happened in real life. Then, when the smoke clears, the audience will see the wreck as it ought to appear — crumpled, wheels off, etc.

One of the problems with a falling object such as the car is that in actual filming of a real-life accident, each movie frame would be slightly blurred. If you are painstaking enough, you can improve the result by deliberately blurring each image. You could use a slow exposure and very slight movement during the time the camera shutter was open. I suggest you use 1/10 sec. if you are shooting the animated series with a 35mm still camera, and very slight movement downward during the actual exposure. If you are using a movie camera and normal speed, then, since the exposure will be only about 1/30 sec., the movement would have to be slightly more pronounced. Expect to make a mess of things the first time around. Be patient. There is no reason why you cannot come up with some very good results once you get the knack. It takes practice and ingenuity.

In the case of explosions I'd suggest you simply run your camera at its fastest speed and literally let the chips fall where they may. With explosions, I attempt to work on as large a scale as possible, because the larger the objects are, the more realistic the explosion will look. It is entirely possible, of course, to work with two or more different scales, using the largest scales for explosion and crash scenes only. You can often use extremely miniature scales (such as HO, 1:86) for the long shots. The larger replica of the miniature could be much more crude as you could cut in to a closer shot, so that the replica would only be shown just as the explosion starts. As soon as you have allowed time for an impressive explosion to expend itself fully, you could then move back to longer-distance scenes showing the miniature amid great smoke and ruin. You could also toss some debris — scale rocks, soil, etc. — in the right directions in front of the camera to simulate the delayed landing of the parts blown highest. Again, use the fastest speed on your movie camera to slow up the travel of debris and particles coming out of the explosion. Gradually the ruins of the miniature set (which you can alter, between scenes, to match the destruction in the larger set) would appear as the smoke gradually cleared from the scene. With excellent cutting and editing, you will be surprised what can be accomplished.

Incidentally, cut-away flashes — ultra-short scenes in which some large object is caught hurtling through space or some person is shown screaming, being hit by some debris — and many other cut-ins and cut-aways may be artfully introduced so that the explosion does not have to be shown as one continuous action. This gives you tremendous latitude, of course. The way to handle this is to shoot all your explosion scenes as continuous footage. Then, later, in editing the film, you can splice in the best action cut-ins and cut-aways at various appropriate points during the explosion. You may have to leave short lengths of the explosion out to compensate, approximately, for other film lengths that you are adding into your film. This is because time continuity must not be fouled up. The audience must feel as though everything takes place in the time it would take for a straight scene of the explosion, from beginning to end, to be run off. You must also maintain the tempo of the explosion, even if your camera turns away from it for an instant. It is much like the measure of a fast song: you must keep the beat. You must not switch from a rock-and-roll's fast pace to a waltz tempo. In the case of the explosion, you must maintain that ultra-fast tempo throughout.

In most cases, you can easily work out how many frames you will need to show something falling a known distance if you know how long it takes the object to fall the distance in real life. Remember the story of Galileo simultaneously dropping two objects, one much larger and heavier than the other, off the Tower of Pisa, and how they reached the ground at the same time. With most of the things with which you will work, you do not have to worry about the factor of wind resistance, so a simple formula will allow you to find how much time it takes an object to fall a known distance. It is as follows:

$$\text{Time (to fall the distance)} = \sqrt{\frac{\text{distance (object falls)}}{4}}$$

Thus, the time it takes a real object to fall a real distance equals the square root of the real distance divided by four. Let's go back to the real cliff, which is 120 feet high. The square root of 120 is approximately 11 ($11 \times 11 = 121$). Divide 11 by 4 and you will get 2.7 seconds. If you remember, we estimated that it would take an actual car, plunging off a 120-foot high cliff, three seconds to hit the ground. It would have taken that car 2.7 seconds if it fell in a plumb line, straight down. But we figured a fast-moving car would project itself forward off the edge of the cliff and then would arc down; we allowed 0.3 second for the resultant trajectory and variance from plumb-line free fall. So, you see, this formula checks out our prior calculations perfectly. You must learn, of

Plumb Line Distance of Free Fall	Approx. Time of Descent	Length of Film 24 fps, 16mm	16 fps,* 8mm	No. of Individual Frames 24 fps†	16 fps‡
25 ft.	1.25 sec.	0.75 ft.	0.25 ft.	30 frames	20 frames
50 ft.	1.8 sec.	1.08 ft.	0.36 ft.	43 frames	29 frames
100 ft.	2.5 sec.	1.50 ft.	0.50 ft.	60 frames	40 frames
200 ft.	3.5 sec.	2.10 ft.	0.70 ft.	84 frames	56 frames
300 ft.	4.3 sec.	2.58 ft.	0.86 ft.	103 frames	69 frames
500 ft.	5.6 sec.	3.36 ft.	1.12 ft.	134 frames	90 frames
1000 ft.	8.0 sec.	4.8 ft.	1.6 ft.	192 frames	128 frames
2000 ft.	11.2 sec.	6.72 ft.	2.24 ft.	268 frames	179 frames
10,000 ft.	25.0 sec.	15.00 ft.	5.0 ft.	600 frames	400 frames

SUPER 8mm = 72 frames per foot
8mm = 80 frames per foot
16mm = 40 frames per foot

*Regular 8mm film was used as a standard here because it is the film that has exactly twice as many frames to the foot as 16mm film. The number of single frames per foot are as follows:

†16mm was figured at 24 frames per second, as that is professional sound-on-film speed. This figure also relates most directly to videotape (if the film were to be used for TV).

‡8mm was figured at 16 frames per second, as that was the old silent speed that was normal for regular 8mm. Some Super 8mm cameras operate normally at 18 frames per second; so if you are using a Super 8mm camera and wish to be a little more accurate, add two frames for each second of time the real object would descend. These figures can only be approximations, since the object will accelerate as it gets closer to the ground. You must, therefore, have more frames per second at the beginning of the fall and fewer toward the end of it. It will take some experimentation to get this just right.

Fig. 6-7

course, to temper the purely mathematical answer with such variances as occur in the natural behavior of objects.

Once you know the number of seconds a free-falling object will take to reach the ground, you will know how long the scene should last on the screen to approximate the normal recording of a falling object in real life. From this, you can calculate how many frames you would have shot, and you can estimate how many single frames you should shoot in making motion pictures (or still shots) of your miniature. For your convenience, I am including a table to enable you to check your own findings.

Far easier to film than free-falling objects, explosions, and the like, is the forward progress of such things as model railroad trains. If the train is just passing static scenery, that is, areas in which nothing in the background moves, then you may simply run the model train past the camera under its own power, regulating its speed by eye and transformer control. However, if there are other objects that might normally move (such as people and animals), then you may wish to animate the train's travel and the other mobile objects.

Of course, the figures you would normally use will not have movable limbs, because the scale figures supplied through hobby shops to go with HO and other such model setups are fixed-limb, statue-like objects. You can usually get

Fig. 6-8a

Fig. 6-8b

Fig. 6-8c

Fig. 6-8d

Fig. 6-8e

Fig. 6-8f

Fig. 6-8g

Fig. 6-8h

by with these, since the audience's attention will be focused on the main foreground action (in this case, the train). As long as the figures move at a natural pace in the background and do nothing to draw particular attention to themselves, chances are the general movement and the progress of these objects will add all the touch of background realism you'll need.

In Fig. 6-7, another section of my basement set is being utilized. My Piolite plastic reflectors come in handy for simulating open, skylight softening of foreground shadows. The antique train is moving, at this point, past some cows and a woman with a wheelbarrow (Fig. 6-8a). There are also some horses in the background. I am not going to show you each individual picture that might have been taken with the single-frame device, or with a still camera, in order to produce animation in this scene. The number of frames would depend upon the speed at which you wished the train to travel. The further it is moved between each frame, the faster it will go forward; the less it is moved between each frame, the slower will be its forward progress.

If the pictures in Fig. 6-8 were the only pictures in the animated film, then there would be a definite error. Can you pick it out? The answer is that the piston rod (the part that turns the wheels) is in the same position in each shot! This is something you must remember: everything that would normally move should be moved to the natural degree between each frame of animation. Thus, not only must you move the train forward, but the wheels should also rotate in a natural manner. To appear natural, the wheels should be advanced to coincide with how their rotation would appear in real life.

You may even wish to blur the wheels of the locomotive if you move in for a close-up of the locomotive itself. You can accomplish this by putting a thin coat of light oil (which must be removed with benzine or a dry-cleaning fluid when you are done) on the track, so that the wheels will slip easily. The oil should be used most sparingly, as you do not want it to spread around. You just want a very thin film on the top of the rail. Have someone, out of sight on one of the back cars, hold the train so it does not move, or pin the train down with black thread. Then have someone turn the electricity quickly on and off during the single-frame exposure. This would cause the wheels to spin and blur, as they might appear in a close-up of an actual locomotive.

In Fig. 6-8, note the progress not only of the train, but also of the woman with the wheelbarrow and of the figures in the far background. Though you hardly notice these figures, a real-life action is introduced, even though the limbs of the figures cannot be moved. The woman with the wheelbarrows, next to the large boulder at the right of the picture, proceeds to a point with the barrow, then leaves it, and moves toward the extreme right edge of the picture. While some of the cows and horses in the background are lying down or at rest, others seem to move about due to slight repositioning of them between frames. The main purpose of Fig. 6-8 is to show you clearly that in a motion-picture film the factor that creates the illusion of movement involves each individual still picture on a strip of movie film showing a slightly advanced stage of action.

If you like doing animation, I will give you a suggestion worth its weight in gold. Go to a professional motion-picture studio, or write to one. Tell them that you wish to make studies of animation and that you would like some discarded film clips of real-life action. List the things you are studying, such as

136

airplanes, race cars, ordinary cars, and boats. Be specific. Tell them you'd like to study just how far these things advance in each frame of movie film. Try to get 35mm motion-picture scraps, which are large enough to study just by holding them up to the light. Ask what they would charge to send such clips to you. You may find it will cost less than it would cost you to shoot your own tests. If you have a friend with a 16mm camera, he may even have discarded clips of various types of action that he would be glad to give to you. The point is, the best way to duplicate any live action is to look at a movie of that action and note carefully how much the action advances in each frame. This is, after all, exactly what you are attempting to duplicate.

There are many other tricks that may be employed. For example, when you are animating a locomotive as in Fig. 6-8, it is desirable to have smoke coming out of the funnel (many models have funnels into which you drop a liquid or pill that creates smoke). But the smoke will not travel back in a natural manner over the train, because the train is not moving forward at the time of the exposure. You can overcome this by sticking medical cotton in the funnel, and using a pair of tweezers to pull it out and back over the train. In each more advanced shot, the cotton would be pulled further back over the locomotive (as though it were real smoke being blown back). You could also add little wisps of cotton coming out of the smoke stack and to the smoke going out over the train. It will take some experimentation to get this right, but it should be well worth the effort.

Much of the success in miniature animation photography will be entirely up to you and your ingenuity. The pros have used all sorts of tricks. For example, to simulate water flowing, sometimes heavier, more viscous fluids are used, such as oil and glycerin. Sometimes the artificial water is not a liquid at all; waterfall effects can be created by mixing flour with marble dust or granulated sugar and letting the mixture pour over a miniature cliff through a burst dam. Also, hundreds of strips of cellophane or other thin, clear plastic may be overlapped and fastened one over the other across an inclined board. These are attached firmly enough so that they will lift up only a fraction of an inch when a wind hits them. By directing a fan or other wind source against the board, the cellophane will flutter and will create a glistening effect of water shimmering in the distance. Backlighting is also used for this effect.

While there are many ways to overcome problems, animation does have some very bad obstacles. One of the toughest problems is duplicating the action of ships in water. The scale of the ship can be reduced, but you just can't reduce the scale of the water. If you employ a fan to create waves in a tub of water into which a miniature ship has been placed, the ship will bob around like a cork, not like a ship. (This is why professionals work with large-size replicas when doing movies of ships in water.) The bobbing of a model ship might be damped by attaching threads fore and aft and dropping them to a submerged wheeled weight, attached by thin rubber bands. By pulling the wheeled weight slowly along a flat bottom, so that the ship would move forward through the water, a simulated heaviness might be imparted to the craft through the damping of its pitch and roll. Again, it would help tremendously to have film clips of the action you are trying to simulate.

We have been talking mainly about animating completely still objects; there is another facet of animation — animation of moving objects, that is, the speeding-up of things progressing normally, so that they will move faster than normal. This is accomplished by running your camera slower than the speed at which the film will be projected. A good many cameras do not have a speed below their normal operating one, but the following table is for those readers who have cameras with slower-than-normal film speeds. I will use 24 frames per second as normal in this instance, as that is professional sound-on-film speed. If you are using 8mm cameras which film normally at either 18 or 16 frames per second, some quick calculation will determine the corresponding speed for your own camera.

Boosting Auto Speed by Slowing Up Camera Speed

Speed of car (24 fps)	Approximate speed of car when camera operated at:			
	20 fps	18 fps	16 fps	8 fps
6 mph	8 mph	9 mph	10 mph	18 mph
10 mph	12 mph	15 mph	17 mph	30 mph
20 mph	25 mph	30 mph	35 mph	60 mph
30 mph	37 mph	45 mph	52 mph	90 mph
40 mph	50 mph	60 mph	70 mph	120 mph
50 mph	62 mph	75 mph	87 mph	150 mph
60 mph	75 mph	90 mph	105 mph	180 mph

There are many times when speeding up the action can be applied to motion pictures of things other than cars, ships, and planes. For example, suppose you wish to show someone having a difficult time swimming in rapids. By having the subject swim more slowly than normal and by using a slow film speed, the subject's action would appear normal while the water would appear more turbulent.

Remember: When the camera runs more slowly than normal, subject action is speeded up. When the camera runs more quickly than normal, subject action is slowed down. This is the secret to many special effects that fall into the category of animation.

Old-time, silent motion pictures have that jerky racing about of figures when they are shown on modern sound-on-film projectors because today's sound projectors run at 24 frames per second and the old-time movie cameras, made for silent projectors, which run at 16 frames per second, exposed film at 16 frames per second. If you projected old silents at 16 frames per second, the action would appear normal. Thus it is possible to make an old-time movie today by running your camera at a speed slower than that at which the finished film will be projected.

A number of professional 16mm cameras are now equipped with various camera speeds. In fact, my trusty old Bell & Howell 70DA, the same type of camera I used all through World War II, has camera speeds of 8, 12, 16, 24, 32, 48, and 64 frames per second. Before purchasing a new camera you should always look into what Bell & Howell, Bolex, Eastman Kodak, Fairchild, Argus, and many other old names in the photographic field are offering. You should investigate their capabilities with special thoroughness if you are interested in trick photography and animation.

Time-Lapse Photography

Before we leave the exciting area of animation, we should talk about time-lapse photography, which is a sophisticated, and often animated, segment of animation. Through time-lapse motion pictures, very slow movements and slow changes of color are made vividly apparent and dramatic. The growth of a plant, the setting of the sun, the construction of a bridge or building are just a few of the examples.

To achieve such an effect, connect a cable release to an 8mm motion-picture camera and make one single-frame exposure every ten minutes. The result will be a flower blooming and wilting, or a building magically springing up stories, in the space of minutes or even seconds.

Time-lapse photography can be made manually, but it is more economical and accurate if the individual exposures are made automatically with equal intervals between each frame. The Pacer III is an automatic exposure device. It is manufactured by UneCO, Bellevue, Nebr. 68005. The Pacer III converts timed electrical impulses into mechanical thrusts to operate the shutter of a motion-picture camera via a cable release. In Fig. 6-9, a Pacer III is shown with the cable release running from it to the threaded cable-release hole in the starting button of the Bell & Howell Super 8mm camera. I suggest you write the maker of this particular device and get full information on it if you should be interested in any type of time-lapse photography.

While spring-driven movie cameras may be used, as long as you remember to wind them up frequently enough, the ideal companion to the Pacer III and other automatic time-lapse devices is, of course, the electric-drive movie camera. What kind of camera you get will depend largely upon the major use to which the film will be put. You might check to see if you may pick up a used 35mm motion picture, or used 16mm motion picture camera with either spring-drive or electric-motor drive that could be adapted to use with a device such as the Pacer III.

Animation is such an intriguing field that we can only scratch its surface in this book; but we have gone far enough so that you now know how it works. This is a field of great individual creativity and personal ingenuity. You can only be given basic guidelines, the fundamentals: time, experimentation, patience, individual creativity and ingenuity, experience, trial and error give you the rest. The field has no limits to either problems or possibilities!

Fig. 6-9

139

7

Titles

Because of their awe of the visual power of the projected picture, most amateurs and some professionals overlook opportunities to employ the written word in a form of title. Titles make almost any motion-picture presentation look better. Many times it is not that titles are necessary for the film to be understood; in fact, that should not be the case. But titles do interpose a relief from a fully pictorial run of scenes. Titles can provide a most enjoyable framing of a sequence, and often inject a certain change of pace into viewing.

Even if you are using sound in conjunction with slides or are putting sound on your film or videotape, your first step is to understand that all pictorial presentations, still or motion, are really picture stories. As such, they must have divisions just as a book has paragraphs and chapters. The problems are where to put the dividers and how to avoid overdoing them.

I think the easiest way to know when to use a title is to stop and meditate what a title is for and why you might try to utilize one at a certain point in a motion-picture presentation. The problem in many pictorial presentations is that one becomes so absorbed in the medium that the basic purpose of the presentation — the best possible communication to others — is lost in the glamour of pictorialism, background music, and commentary. The pause that refreshes, the contrast that enhances — the title — is forgotten. To avoid this pitfall, think of each scene or picture (in a slide show) as a visual sentence; each group of scenes as a visual paragraph; and each group of sequences as a visual chapter.

This line of reasoning simplifies matters, does it not? Where you would italicize, underline, or otherwise emphasize a written sentence might be an area in which a title could be used. Where you might emphasize a paragraph beginning, you might consider a title. It all depends upon how specifically explanatory your presentation is supposed to be and how frequently continuity of thought would necessitate a title. In general, where the pictorial presentation is to be more entertaining than directly instructional, you would relate its make-up to the layout of an entertaining book in which few italics or other means of emphasis are used and the main headings are between chapters. These titles, which head each chapter, serve any of the following purposes: to introduce a new line of thought; to effect a transition from one line of thought to another; to establish a concept or an anticipation of what will follow; or to maintain continuity. Of course, there may be other purposes, but usually the object of a good chapter heading in an entertaining book is one or a combination of the foregoing. Whichever your purpose — introductory, transitional, mood-setting, or continuity-maintaining — use titles only when they contribute effectively to enjoyment and understanding.

Signs for Titles

Now, with this fundamental knowledge clearly in our minds, we are ready to tackle the how of title-making. Often making entertaining and enhancing titles is as easy as taking candy from a baby. In your travels, for example, you are literally surrounded by ready-made, easily photographed, natural titles. The entrances to a highway, national park, or zoo are often marked with attractive signs. These are physically so large that you do not have a problem with parallax or ultra-close focus. Try, however, to put your camera on a tripod, especially when shooting motion pictures, as camera movement during a title scene is much more noticeable than in any ordinary scene.

In motion pictures, make title scenes much longer than you think necessary. If you are not producing special effects in the camera, this extra footage allows you to have optical effects put on by a lab. If you wish to do these effects yourself, purchase some "blooping ink" and paint out either the left or right side of the film to an increasing degree. As you black out less and less of the scene in each successive frame of movie film, the title will come more and more into view. You can also cause the scene to disappear gradually by blocking out more and more of the scene, with ink, in each successive frame.

Blooping ink is used to block out parts of sound tracks on movie film. If your local photo dealer does not carry it, write to a motion-picture laboratory dealing in the printing of sound films or to Eastman Kodak, and I am sure they will be able to provide you with the name of a source. India ink should not be used, as it and most other paints and inks are too brittle when dry and crack with the continuous flexing of the film. Hand-painting various designs gives you an endless array of easy-to-do special effects for beginnings and ends of scenes.

At this point you may be asking, how long should I run the camera when shooting a title? A good many people read the sign while shooting and stop shooting when they have finished reading it, thinking this is long enough. They forget that the title that pops on the screen is strange and unfamiliar to the audience. As a rule, hold the starting button down long enough for you to read through the title twice without hurrying. If you are going to have special effects at the beginning and/or end of the title, the sections to be treated must be shot as extra footage. Always assume that the audience will not be able to read the title except during the time it is on the screen without a special effect. For 8mm film, the minimum footage for these extra lengths should be six inches each. At 16 to 18 frames per second, six inches takes up $2\frac{1}{2}$ sec. of screen time. For 16mm film, the minimum footage should be one foot. At 24 frames per second, one foot takes up $1\frac{2}{3}$ sec. of screen time. The total extra footage per title scene, with special effects at both beginning and end, should be about two feet in 16mm and one foot in 8mm. If you do not have a film-counter on your camera and intend to put special effects at both beginning and end, you can follow this procedure. Count aloud: "One thousand and one, one thousand and two, one thousand." Then read the words included in your title twice. Finally, count aloud again: "One thousand and one, one thousand and two, one thousand." If you are ever in doubt about length, make it longer. You can always cut the scene when editing.

The next obvious question is, How large should the lettering be? You will have to decide how close you must get to the sign. The simplest method of deciding this is to get close enough so that the letters of the title are exceptionally legible to you as you film the title. Thus, in asking you to read the title twice as you shoot it, I have forced you to place yourself at the proper distance from what you are filming. When in doubt, move in closer.

When you set up to project your slides, motion pictures, or videotape, the following table will be useful. It is for white letters on a black background, so if you have colored letters on a colored background or letters less legible in design, they should be projected larger than the chart indicates. If letters of different sizes are used, apply the chart to the smallest size. If the smallest is legible, everything else will be.

If you are projecting a distance of:	The smallest letters or symbols should be this high:
128 ft.	4 in.
64 ft.	2 in.
32 ft.	1 in.
16 ft.	½ in.
8 ft.	¼ in.

Other Special Titles

In addition to signs of all sorts, there are many other ready-made titles available in magazines, advertisements, travel folders, newspaper headlines, maps, and so on. Nor is it necessary for you to have a "titler" in order to shoot many other title scenes. You can even draw a variety of letters or even sketches in sand or snow. Just be sure to shoot at a time of day when the light hits the sand or snow at an oblique angle (morning or afternoon). You want whatever indentations you make to contrast well with the light-colored background. This is an instance in which your Pola-Screen may prove useful in cutting glare and improving texture rendition.

A blackboard and chalk can often be used to make informal titles. If you wish to get tricky about it, you can make the lettering appear as if it were being written by an invisible hand. Just single-frame the whole thing. Make one little mark on the blackboard at the start of the first letter about one-inch long. Expose a single frame of this. Continue the mark another half an inch. Expose another single frame. Do this with each letter until, frame by frame, you have formed every letter in every word. When you project all these frames, a chalk line will magically appear on the blackboard and flow into forming each word until the message is complete. You should, of course, run a little film with the blackboard blank at the beginning and, after the single-framing has completed the message, allow the camera to run for about another second or so.

Another very effective title trick is to have a wave wash a shell bearing the title up on shore. To do this, you need two nearly identical shells. The message is painted on one of them with water-resistant paint. Toss the untitled one onto the sand in an almost receded wave, so that what is left of the wave will tumble the shell past the camera lens or will wash over it and leave it glistening in the sand. Before the water clears entirely stop your camera. With it stopped, either zoom in for a close-up of the shell or move the camera as close as possible. Have someone hold the unpainted shell in place with one hand. When you have it all framed and focused, replace the unpainted shell with the titled shell, printed side facing the camera. Wait for a wave to come in and, while the water is still receding, start your camera to catch the last part of the receding wave passing over the title on the prepared shell. Let the camera run; once the water has cleared away, let the camera run long enough for you to read the title over twice. When you project this film, it will appear as though a shell with the title inscribed on it was washed in from the ocean.

An excellent and natural transitional shot is now automatically set up for you. If you time the waves properly, you'll probably just finish shooting the title when another wave will come along and cover up the title shell. When this happens, you can blur the scene a bit by throwing your lens slightly out of focus. Once the scene is blurred, you may then stop your camera, move it, and get set for your next scene — possibly of someone trying to get wet in the cold water. Get everything nicely framed (with the camera in focus). Throw your camera out of focus before you start it. If you have a zoom lens, make sure it is set for the desired field of view. Start the camera and come into focus on the first scene of your movie. (Don't go past the point of focus!) Once in focus, let the scene run out. All this must, of course, require a tripod so that the framing does not jump around while the camera is off.

This technique of focus-to-blur at a scene end, followed by a blur-to-focus at the beginning of the following scene, is an excellent transition that may be used not only between title and scene, but also as a substitute for lap dissolves, wipes, swish-pans, and other special effects. As with all effects, watch your step. Try to use the effect that best fits the scenes between which you intend to introduce it. Effects must contribute to continuity even though the effect itself may be pictorially unclear. The only time you might depart from this rule is when you are making a film that is deliberately fast-paced and disjointed. Even then, believe it or not, there must be a certain rhythm to the irregularity.

There is an endless array of possibilities for title material everywhere you look, everywhere you go. Rocks, driftwood, boxes, cans, and many other readily available things will take lettering nicely. Don't, however, put lettering on property from which you cannot remove it or effectively cover it up. Permanently defacing buildings, trees, walls, and the like are a disgrace to your profession. As an artist and a creator of beauty, you should never be responsible for making our world ugly.

143

Close-up Lenses

Close-up lenses are often used for making titles. I am including, therefore, a Kodak Customer Service Department pamphlet (#AD-30), reprinted by permission. It contains all the information necessary for using close-up lenses in formal titles (as opposed to "found" titles).

When you're watching a movie, it's exciting to see the screen suddenly filled with a close-up picture of a small subject such as a flower, a butterfly, or a model railroad engine. Close-up movies are exciting — and fun, too, especially when they're your movies. Best of all, close-up movies are really easy to make.

Most 8mm and Super 8mm movie cameras allow you to make sharp movies no closer than about 3½ feet from your subject. To get really big pictures of small subjects, this just isn't close enough. You can get closer by putting an inexpensive close-up lens over your camera lens. Close-up lenses, like filters, come in different sizes (series) to fit different camera lenses. With most cameras you will also need an adapter ring to hold the close-up lens in place. Usually your camera manual will tell you what series close-up lens your camera accepts and what adapter ring your camera needs, if any. Your photo dealer can also measure your camera lens to tell you what series close-up lens and what adapter ring you need. . . .

Subject Distance Is Critical

When you make close-up movies, its important that you measure the distance to your subject quite accurately. That's because depth of field is very small when the camera is very close to the subject. Also, unless you, have a camera with a reflex viewfinding system, the viewfinder on your camera will not be accurate enough at close ranges. That's because the viewfinder is some distance above (or to the side of) the camera lens and therefore doesn't "see" exactly the same area the camera lens "sees." (You don't have this problem with a reflex camera, because when you look through the viewfinder you are looking directly through the lens.) At normal shooting distances, this variance is so slight that it can be ignored. But at very close distances, parallax becomes a very important consideration.

Fortunately, it's easy to make a cardboard measuring device to measure the subject distance as well as indicate the picture area. You can make one from a piece of cardboard such as laundries put into shirts. Consult the appropriate table to find the distance to the subject and the field size for your combination of camera and close-up lens. Then cut the cardboard as shown in Fig 7-1.* You will need a different cardboard measuring device for each close-up lens, because the subject distance and picture area vary, depending on the close-up lens you use. If your camera has a focusing lens, be sure to note the distance for which it should be set.

---

*Some cameras, usually 16mm, require that the subject distance be measured from the film plane rather than from the close-up lens. The film plane is usually marked by a ϕ on the camera body just behind the lens. If this is true of your camera, cut out the end of the cardboard that fits against the camera so that the edge of the cardboard is even with the film-plane indicator on the camera.

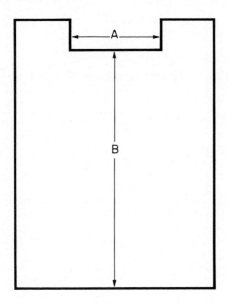

Fig. 7-1

Dimension	3+ lens		2+ lens	
	Super 8mm	Regular 8mm	Super 8mm	Regular 8mm
A	5⅛	4⅜	7½	6⅜
B	12¼	12¼	17¾	17¾

This table gives the measurements (in inches) for a cardboard measuring device for use with either a fixed focus Super 8mm or regular 8mm camera, each equipped with a 13mm lens.

If you have a tripod, it's a good idea to use it for your close-up movies. A tripod makes it easier to hold the camera at the correct subject distance. It also eliminates camera movement, which is much more noticeable in close-ups than in normal movies.

Close-ups with a Zoom Lens

As we said before the important factor in making close-ups with any camera is the subject distance. If you have a close-up lens on a zoom camera and have accurately measured the subject distance, maintain that distance and you can zoom the lens to any position and still get sharp pictures. The subject distance is the same for a specific close-up lens regardless of the focal length of the camera lens. Of course, when you use the wide-angle position you will photograph more of your subject; when you use the telephoto position you will photograph less of your subject.

Depth of field is smaller when the zoom lens is in the telephoto position than when it's in the wide-angle position, so measure the subject distance very accurately if you use the telephoto position. Also, since the depth of field may be even less than one inch, try to keep the subject in one plane parallel to the front of the camera so that as much of the subject as possible will be in the sharpness range.

The data in the following tables is applicable to zoom lenses. For example, the data for a 36mm lens on a Super 8mm camera applies to a zoom lens on a Super 8mm camera when the lens is in the 36mm position; the data for a 12mm lens applies when the zoom lens is in the 12mm position. and so on.

Data on Close-up Lenses

Fixed-Focus Super 8mm Camera with 13mm Lens

2+ Close-up Lens		3+ Close-up Lens	
Close-up Lens-to-Subject Distance (inches)	Approximate Field Size (inches)	Close-up Lens-to-Subject Distance (inches)	Approximate Field Size (inches)
17¾	5⅝ × 7½	12¼	3¾ × 5⅛

Super 8mm Camera with Focusing Lens

Lens	Camera Focus Setting (feet)	2+ Close-up Lens		3+ Close-up Lens	
		Close-up Lens-to-Subject Distance (inches)	Approximate Field Size (inches)	Close-up Lens-to-Subject Distance (inches)	Approximate Field Size (inches)
9.5mm	inf.	19½	8½ × 11¾	13	5⅝ × 7⅝
	25	18½	8 × 11	12½	5⅜ × 7⅜
	10	16⅞	7⅜ × 10	11⅞	5⅛ × 7
	6	15½	6¾ × 9⅛	11⅛	4¾ × 6½
12mm	inf.	19½	6⅝ × 9⅛	13	4⅜ × 6
	25	18½	6⅜ × 8⅝	12½	4¼ × 5¾
	10	16⅞	5¾ × 7⅝	11⅞	4 × 5½
	6	15½	5¼ × 7¼	11⅛	3¾ × 5⅛
36mm	inf.	19½	2⅛ × 2⅞	13	1⅜ × 1⅞
	25	18½	2 × 2¾	12½	1¼ × 1¾
	10	16⅞	1⅞ × 2½	11⅞	1¼ × 1⅝
	6	15½	1⅝ × 2¼	11⅛	1⅝ × 1½
45mm	inf.	19½	1⅝ × 2¼	13	1 × 1½
	25	18½	1½ × 2⅛	12½	1 × 1⅜
	10	16⅞	1⅜ × 1⅞	11⅞	1 × 1¼
	6	15½	1¼ × 1¾	11⅛	⅞ × 1¼

146

Fixed-Focus Regular 8mm Camera with 13mm Lens

2+ Close-up Lens		3+ Close-up Lens	
Close-up Lens-to-Subject Distance (inches)	Approximate Field Size (inches)	Close-up Lens-to-Subject Distance (inches)	Approximate Field Size (inches)
17¾	4⅝ × 6⅜	12¼	3⅛ × 4⅜

Regular 8mm Camera with Focusing Lens

Lens	Camera Focus Setting (feet)	Close-up Lens-to-Subject Distance (inches)	Approximate Field Size (inches)	Close-up Lens-to-Subject Distance (inches)	Approximate Field Size (inches)
	inf.	19½	7½ × 10¼	13	5 × 6¾
9mm	25	18½	7 × 9⅝	12½	4¾ × 6½
	10	16⅞	6⅜ × 8⅞	11⅞	4½ × 6⅛
	6	15½	6 × 8	11⅛	3⅝ × 5
	inf.	19½	5 × 6¾	13	3⅜ × 4½
13mm	25	18½	4¾ × 6⅜	12½	3¼ × 4⅜
	10	16⅞	4⅜ × 5⅞	11⅞	3⅛ × 4⅛
	6	15½	4 × 5⅜	11⅛	2⅞ × 3⅞
	inf.	19½	2⅜ × 3¼	13	1-9/16 × 2⅛
27mm	25	18½	2¼ × 3⅛	12½	1½ × 2-1/16
	10	16⅞	2-1/16 × 2-13/16	11⅞	1⅜ × 1-15/16
	6	15½	1⅞ × 2-9/16	11⅛	1⅜ × 1⅞

16mm Camera with Kodak Cine Ektar Lens, 25mm f/1.9 or 25mm f/1.4
(Subject distance measured to film plane.)

	2+ Close-up Lens		3+ Close-up Lens	
Camera Focus Setting (inches)	Subject-to-Film Plane Distance (inches)	Approximate Field Size (inches)	Subject-to-Film Plane Distance (inches)	Approximate Field Size (inches)
24	Close-up lens not needed;		11⅜	2⅜ × 3¼
20	use focusing adjustment.		10⅝	2¼ × 2
16	11⅛	2¼ × 3	9⅞	1 × 2½
12	9½	1 × 2½	8½	1¾ × 2¼

Standard Titling

Before we get into making our own titles, I think it wise to mention in passing that there are many stock titles that are already shot and available in various lengths of film, such as "The End," "Happy New Year," "Happy Birthday," "Merry Christmas," and the like. Again, I refer you to *The Photo-Dealer Directory* and Eastman Kodak Customer Service for suppliers of these titles as well as for names of organizations who will make up titles to order.

Fig. 7-2b

Fig. 7-2a

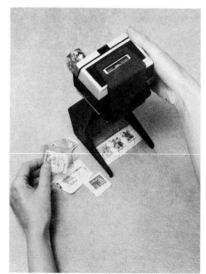

Fig. 7-3

For titling with slides, Kodak manufactures the Kodak Ektagraphic Visual-maker in Fig. 7-2a. This kit is complete with camera, two different stands, and other accessories you need in order to take slides. Figures 7-2b and 7-3 show the camera in use on the different stands in order to photograph different material. These stands would give the cinematographer a choice of two sizes of titles. The stand shown in Fig. 7-2b is an 8″ × 8″ copy stand suitable for photographing prints, drawings, reproductions of paintings, graphs, charts, diagrams, passages of text, titles, flowers, and small animals. The 3″ × 3″ copy

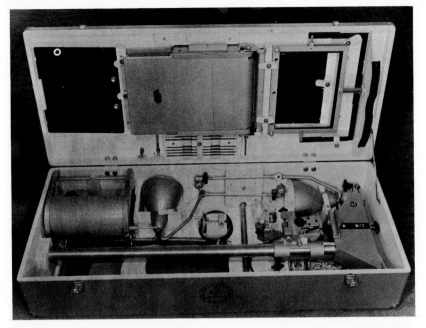

Fig. 7-4

stand shown in Fig. 7-3 is designed for photographing details of a painting, drawing, or map. It can also be used to make pictures of small objects such as coins, stamps, insignias, insects, botanical specimens, and machine parts. There are, of course, many other uses. When using such a device for motion-picture and videotape copying or titling, you will also need photofloods or other lights. There are other simple copy and title setups besides the Kodak model, which you ought to look into before purchasing any.

In Fig. 7-4, you see a professional motion-picture titling kit. This one is the Bolex Super Titler distributed by Paillard Inc., 1900 Lower Rd., Box 564, Linden, N. J. This is one of the most complete and sophisticated titling sets I have seen, short of elaborate, permanent titling equipment. Highly professional results may be obtained with the Bolex outfit for slides, motion pictures, and videotape. The owner's manual supplied with this titling kit is a complete book in itself. It shows in detail how to use the equipment and offers stimulating suggestions for experimentation. The complete array of attachments that comes with this kit makes it extremely flexible. While this outfit is made specifically for Bolex cameras, I doubt that you would have difficulty using other makes with it. Consult with both Bolex and your dealer in regard to this matter before making a purchase if you intend to use other cameras with it. Check out other makes: there may be a better one that I have overlooked. With the Bolex equipment, the title can be slowly moved up and out of the field of view by turning a geared crank, as shown in Fig. 7-5. You can also single-frame the title. One #1 Photoflood was used in each of the reflectors, one to either side of the title, at 45-degree angles.

149

Fig. 7-5

Fig. 7-6

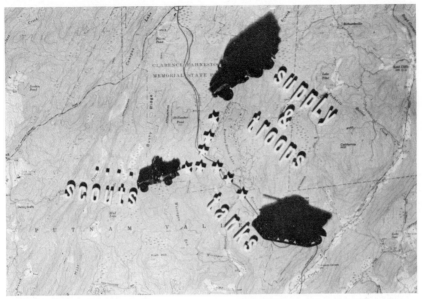

Fig. 7-7

Another item indispensible to titling is a set of white three-dimensional characters that includes capital and lower-case letters, numerals, some punctuation marks, and a few miscellaneous symbols. I use a set of white plaster-type title letters made by Hernard Manufacturing Co., Inc., in Yonkers, N. Y. The kit comes complete in its own plastic case. The letters are of the stick-on type but are rigid. They are about 1/4″ thickness from face to back. The capital letters are about 3/4″ in height and the lower-case letters are more than 1/2″ in height. These are excellent sizes for letters and numbers for 8mm, 16mm, and videotape title characters. In Fig. 7-5, my Bell & Howell Super 8mm camera is being used to film the title letters made by Hernard.

In Fig. 7-6, you see the titler used in a vertical position. This time a different moving-title device is in place. In Fig. 7-5, a round, drumlike arrangement was utilized, which moved the title letters in and out of focus and view more quickly than the oval arrangement shown in Fig. 7-6. In the letter setup, the letters will be in a flat plane for a considerable time, so that they will come in and out of view but will not go in and out of focus. One of the advantages of working with the titler set vertically is that the title letters and other objects will lie in place without any adhesive. It is therefore quicker and easier to introduce, say, chess pieces, as in Fig. 7-6, or other trim or objects that might be related to your title at any time during the filming of the title. This is especially helpful if you are single-framing.

By single-framing, you can animate the title by placing one letter at a time on the title background between the shooting of each frame. If you wish the letters to appear at a slower rate, you may, of course, shoot two or more frames between the placing of each letter. Or you may make whole words pop onto the screen by single-framing between words. In all these cases, you must allow

151

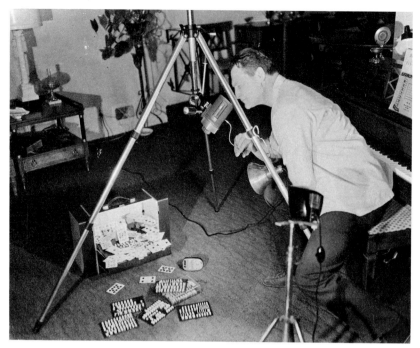

Fig. 7-8

some footage to roll before the words start coming on the screen and let the completed title remain on the screen long enough to be easily read.

In making titles, much depends upon the human element. Figure 7-7 shows that it is possible to take fine three-dimensional letters and, just by lighting them improperly, foul up the whole title. The background here is just a little too weak, especially where the lighting kills the bottom section of the letters.

Reverse Action in Titling

In Fig. 7-8, you will see another trick in titling that may come in handy. The movie camera is in position upside down on an elevator tripod; it is ready to shoot the series in Fig. 7-9. The strip of film shot with the camera in this position can then be cut away from the subsequent scenes. By rotating this strip 180 degrees, always keeping the shiny, non-emulsion side up, and splicing the head of this strip to the head of the next scene, one would then have a title sequence with the action reversed, but with the images right side up and not reversed from left to right. This works because the original film was shot upside down and reversed from left to right though the action was not reversed. Turning the film around and resplicing it alters each of these characteristics.

This trick works best with 16mm film (although an 8mm camera is shown in Fig. 7-8), because 16mm film has sprocket holes along both edges. With

8mm and Super 8mm film, one would have to flip the film strip, in the course of the above procedure, and splice the title sequence with the *emulsion* side up in order to get the sprocket holes back on the right side. This places the image in a slightly different plane in relation to the projector lens and results in a slightly out-of-focus screen image.

With 8mm film, you have two more practical alternatives than flipping the film; both involve shooting the scene with the camera in its normal upright position. One alternative is simply to send the film to an optical printing lab and have the action reversed through optical printing. By the other method, you can shoot the scene straight, reverse it in the projector, and film as it is rear-projected on a process screen. This would be fine as long as there was no lettering involved. If you want all lettering and action to appear in proper relation, you would use front-projection and film the scene you wished to reverse with your projector running backwards.

There are many uses for reverse action in titling. The series in Fig. 7-9 is an example. The entire sequence was filmed as follows: The title words and playing cards are arranged on the turntable of a phonograph. With the camera running upside down "CARDS ARE TRICKY" is read over twice, for timing. With the camera still running, the turntable is turned on. It revolves slowly at first, then quickly, throwing the cards off the wheel. At the end of the scene, the cards would be thoroughly scattered.

When this scene is turned around, spliced into place, and projected, the title would appear as follows: Scattered cards would fly up and onto the turntable, aligning themselves around the title words. If any of the letters had spun off, they, too, would pop back onto the turntable, in proper place. At the end of the scene the cards and words would be in exactly the right position. The title would remain still for a time so it could be read.

Fig. 7-9

I think Fig. 7-9 will give you an excellent idea of just what you do to reverse action. The strip of film is shown as it would be in the camera, upside down with left-to-right reversal. To view these frames as the scene should be spliced and projected, turn this book upside down. Now the scene becomes right side up. The jumble of cards is in proper place as it would be the end of the scene. The last picture represents not just one frame, but about 72 identical single frames at the end of the scene, when the audience is absorbing the title. Just as you rotated the book 180 degrees to see how this works, so would you rotate the actual scene on 16mm film in order to create reversed action in projection.

No matter what kind of motion pictures you may shoot, I'm sure you will be able to use reverse action from time to time, not just for titles, but also special effects and trick photography of many types. It certainly is a most useful thing to know about.

Other Kinds of Titles

You must not forget our old friend, the matte box, when doing titles. It is possible to put small letters on a transparent acetate cell or piece of thin, clear glass and put this in place at the farthest possible distance from the lens. The farther away you set it up, the more likely it and the scene beyond are to be in focus simultaneously. Another way of making this would be simply to take a window frame with clear glass, attach large letters to it, and move back still farther away and, therefore, increase your depth of field.

The general rule to remember is that you want your film plane to be exactly parallel with the title face; and the title to be exactly centered in the taking lens. Take care to achieve this alignment except in instances where you feel an angle shot will add something to the title scene. There will be many opportunities in which you may apply many of the other techniques learned in this book to your title-making. Always try to stay alert to anything that will improve your presentation. Use your knowledge, common sense, and imagination. Do not over-title; but remember that often titles can be used for more than just the beginning and end of a film.

8

Sound

Background music, voice commentary, even the sounds of nature or a city location can now be added to motion pictures as easily as you use your tape recorder. I will not go into adding sound to videotape as that, from its inception, is a sound-on-film proposition. With videotape, there is absolutely no problem to taping sound right along with shooting the film. The ways to use sound with videotape and the technique of making sound enhance videotape are so similar to those in motion-picture sound that there is no need to separate the two media in any basic discussion.

Sound with Motion Pictures: Magnetic Sound-Tracks

The various methods of synchronizing sound move the sound-track right along with the film — and this applies, of course, to videotaping as well — thus providing the most accurate and dependable means of being sure the sound you want reaches the audience in synchronization with the related frames. (We will hold off discussing professional "optical" sound-tracks for the moment.) *Magnetic* sound-tracks are most used nowadays in recording — even by professionals, as it is possible to record a magnetic track later onto an optical one. Thus, whether you are going to add sound-on-film to home movies or professional ones, chances are you will record on a magnetic track first.

Various ways are used to add magnetic striping to film. One, Kodak Sono-track Coating, is the brand name for a magnetic coating that can be applied along the edge of exposed and processed 8mm and 16mm motion-picture films. This coating service is available through Kodak dealers and can be placed on either original or duplicates of black-and-white or color films. Once this coating has been applied, either live or previously recorded voice or music can be recorded on the film by using a sound projector designed for magnetic recording as well as magnetic playback. Check out the various manufacturers to see who makes what. Bell & Howell has made a 16mm magnetic sound projector for a number of years that can both record and play magnetic sound. Eastman Kodak makes the 16mm Kodak Pageant Magnetic-Optical Sound Projector as well as the Kodak Sound 8 Projector (for regular 8mm) and the Kodak Instamatic M100 Sound Projector (for Super 8mm), which records and plays back magnetic sound films (Fig. 8-1a).

Fig. 8-1a

Fig. 8-1b

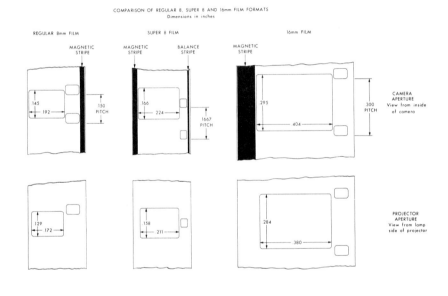

COMPARISON OF REGULAR 8, SUPER 8 AND 16mm FILM FORMATS
Dimensions in inches

REGULAR 8mm FILM	SUPER 8 FILM		16mm FILM

EASTMAN KODAK COMPANY

The wonderful thing about the magnetic system is that you can watch your film being projected and record the sound as the scenes appear on the screen. The film can be rewound and you can hear immediately the sound you just added. If you don't like it, you can erase and re-record, with no more difficulty than if you were working with an ordinary tape recorder. Once the magnetic coating is put on the film, you use that film for recording purposes just as if it were tape in an ordinary tape recorder. The system is amazingly simple to use.

Kodak Sonotrack Coating is applied to the side of the film that faces the projector lamp during projection. Reversal films, all Super 8mm films, and most

156

color films have the coating applied to the base (shiny) side of the film, not to the emulsion (dull) side. The Sonotrack Coating may be applied in three widths: full width (about 0.100 inch) ; half width (about 0.050 inch) ; and quarter width (about 0.030 inch). The quarter width is applied to 8mm films (Fig. 8-1b).

When the half-width magnetic coating is put on a variable area of the optical track, the optical track may become very poor. For the following reasons, I suggest that you make a short section of duplicate of the film (with the same optical track) and have the Sonotrack Coating applied to this section to see exactly how much loss of quality or increase of distortion would result from having the half-width Sonotrack Coating applied over half of the optical track. If this distortion and the resultant quality loss are too great, make a master duplicate of the film. Add the magnetic Sonotrack Coating to this duplicate, and keep the original optical track intact and unmolested. This way you can use either type of track, with best possible fidelity in each.

When you send in 16mm film that is perforated along only one edge to be coated, the coating will be applied on the full width, unless you specify otherwise. If there is an optical track already on the film, a half-width track will be applied, unless otherwise specified. On film with sprocket holes along both edges and on regular 8mm film, the magnetic track is applied along the outside of the perforations. On Super 8mm film, the recording track is put on along the edge opposite the sprocketed edge in quarter width of 0.030 inch, running from the outside edge of the film to the edge of the picture area. A thin dummy stripe is applied to the sprocketed edge of the film, for balance.

Before you send in any film for magnetic coating, carefully inspect all splices to be sure they will hold and not tear, catch, or pull apart as the film is run through the coating machine. Be sure to cut out any bad areas of film such as those that have wrinkles, bad splices, and torn sprocket holes. If you leave such work for the coating laboratory, there will be a charge for it, and processing will be slowed up considerably.

Kodak Sonotrack Coating may be put on to all 8mm and 16mm films at the time they are sent to the Film Processing Laboratory in Rochester for development. However, I suggest the following procedure as being far more professional, efficient, and less costly:

1. Send all the rolls of film on the same topic in for processing; make sure you send them all.

2. When the processed film is returned, edit it carefully.

3. Once the film is roughly edited, inspect all splices and every other part of the film to make sure there are no bad spots.

4. When the film is completely edited (with titles in place and all bad areas cut out), send the film in for sound-striping.

For professional, high-quality sound, it is best to shoot 16mm film that is perforated with sprocket holes along one edge only, so that a full width of track can be applied. Several kinds and lengths of 16mm Eastman and Kodak films are available in this form and cost the same as film with sprocket holes along both edges. You may have to order this film specially, but it is available.

Many professional cameras having double pull-down claws (to insure steadiness) require double-sprocketed film. But this does not mean that you must settle for sound that is second-best. When the film is processed, have a work print made in addition to the original. Then have the work print and original edge-numbered to match each other. Do all your timing of commentary and background music and your editing on the work print. When the final editing and sound-matching is decided on, alter the original to suit your plans. (This procedure saves wear and tear on the original.) Send the original to a duplicating laboratory, and have the master or the release prints (for more restricted use) made on film sprocketed along one edge only. It is to this master that sound will be added.

If you intend to add an optical sound-track before any masters are made, consult the sound recording studio and follow their instructions on how to add a sound-track to masters that already carry a photographic track.

Sonotrack Coating can be applied to masters made on film with sprocket holes along one side only. Since the film is already completely edited, it can be magnetically sound-striped when duplicated. The Sonotrack Coating is, therefore, applied to an edited spliceless strip of film. Adding sound later to the Sonotrack Coating is as simple as using a regular tape recorder. You can, of course, record while your film is run off, but this is not likely to give you professional results.

Today, many professional-type 16mm motion-picture cameras have a single pull-down claw system. Since 1935, Kodak Cine-Specials have the single pull-down claw, as do the Kodak Reflex Special 16mm camera and all models of the Cine Kodak K-100 camera. Along with the single pull-down claw, the film advance system must employ a single set of teeth on all sprocket wheels, which lie, of course, on the same side of the film as the sprocket holes. Many other manufacturers offer advanced cameras with the single-edge sprocket-hole system or offer a conversion service that enables their models having double-sprocket setups to be converted to the single-edge system.

The all-time standard projection speed for sound-on-film motion pictures is 24 frames per second, and the best quality of magnetic sound is reproduced by projecting at this standard speed. However, good-quality sound still may be obtained if you record and project at either 16 or 18 frames per second on the magnetic sound stripe.

Care of Films with Magnetic Sound

Film that has Sonotrack Coating and on which sound has been recorded should be stored with the same precautions used in storing any other motion-picture film. Heat and humidity cause deterioration of the film and, to a certain extent, of the magnetic track. However, as far as is currently known, magnetic sound-track is as permanent as the film base to which the coating has been applied. Storing film having magnetic sound in metal containers or cabinets or on aluminum or steel reels will not adversely affect the recorded sound. One precaution: do not store the film near a permanent magnet or near any electrical wiring carrying a heavy current. Also avoid erasing the magnetic sound-track accidentally by having the projector controls improperly set when you show the film.

158

Before cleaning with a solvent or applying a lacquer to a film on which there is a magnetically recorded sound-track, make a test on a discarded piece of the film to be sure that the solvent in the cleaner or the lacquer itself will not dissolve the binder used in the magnetic strip coating. If the stripe softens or smears, use another type of cleaner or lacquer.

Note: When a film lacquer is used, it should not cover the magnetic stripe. If it does, the sound-track will be raised away from the magnetic head of the projector by the thickness of the layer of lacquer. This increased distance of the magnetic sound-track from the recording and playback heads will cause serious degradation of the high-frequency sound quality.

Magnetic sound-track recording of the type we have been discussing is a real boon to both 8mm and 16mm, as it brings good-quality sound into fields in which the higher cost of optical sound for release prints might be prohibitive. Schools, hobby groups, local TV stations, civic organizations, church groups, business and industry, sporting groups, and last, but not least, the home movie-maker, all are in a position to take full advantage of this simple and low cost method of putting sound on film. Furthermore, 8mm sound, especially on Super 8mm film, will greatly expand creative possibilities. The tremendous versatility of magnetic sound-on-film recording can be of outstanding advantage when the film is needed to serve various types of audiences. For example, think of the great value when the film is to be shown to people who speak different languages (including teen-agers). Magnetic sound makes it possible to adapt a film easily and inexpensively to different types of audiences.

Vital, of course, to good sound-on-film is the instrument with which you record it and the one with which you play it back. I think the Kodak Instamatic M100 Sound Projector, which I use to record and project my Super 8mm motion pictures, is a good example of equipment that is both reliable and simple to use. Its features are those for which you should look in any recording sound projector:

1. *Automatic threading:* runs film through film gate and around the sound head; film then easily attached to take-up reel.

2. *Transistorized sound:* instant sound, no warm-up period; built-in 2″ x 10″ speaker with ample power to work external speakers if you wish to add them.

3. *Easy-to-use recording controls:* record-play switch has push-turn action to prevent accidental erasing of sound-track, once you have recorded it; a red light informs you when projector is set to record; tone control for playback with high fidelity rendition; volume control to adjust sound level.

4. *VU dial for careful volume control:* meter needle shows you volume at which you are recording; you record at peak efficiency with continuing, precise control for fine recording results (Fig. 8-2a).

5. *Alfenol recording head:* Kodak claims this magnetic head is made of a new metal (called "Alfenol") that will record for thousands of hours without loss in sound quality. So far, in my use of their projector, it seems true. Generally speaking, firms like Kodak and Bell & Howell are reliable, and their claims fairly accurate.

6. *Microphone and phono inputs; speaker outlet:* with the two inputs, you can record voices and music separately or at the same time; speaker output

159

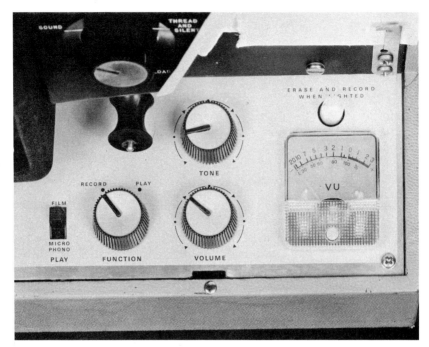

Fig. 8-2a

Fig. 8-2b

160

Fig. 8-2c   Fig. 8-2d

allows you to play back the sound-track through a separate speaker and your own home sound system (in addition to normal sound from projector itself); you can also use projector as a PA system (Figs. 8-2b and 8-2c).

7. *1200-foot capacity reel:* projector comes equipped with a 400-foot take-up reel; optional 1200-foot reels may be used for one-hour viewings; 1200 feet of film can be rewound in less than two minutes.

8. *You may record it either 18 or 24 frames per second.*

9. *Two levels of illumination for projector bulb:* brilliant for showings; lower level (to help preserve bulb) for your own use (Fig. 8-2d).

There are, of course, many other features, but these are some of the outstanding ones that contribute considerably to the utility and ease of operation of the sound recording projector.

If you are going to do much recording, there are three other pieces of equipment you should acquire: a stop-watch, a footage counter, and a tape recorder.

You will need a stop-watch to time scenes. By timing scene lengths you can efficiently trim commentary to a point where much less actual recording will have to take place. You will also be able to select musical background more intelligently, and to fit in the time it takes to project the scene with which the music will be used.

A footage counter indicates the amount of footage that has passed through it from the feed reel to the take-up reel. It helps you to determine exact lengths of scenes and to locate specific scenes by edge-number. It should have at least two synchronized sets of sprocket wheels, so that an original and a master, or a master and any other dupe, may be run along together, side by side, when desired, and matched to each other. A footage counter is also used in conjunction with matching the original to the work print and to other masters and prints, when necessary. It is of tremendous aid when trying to make sure com-

161

mentary and music will match the film at any given point, and is often used in matching an optical track to the film.

You may also find you need a tape recorder. The type would depend upon the kind of work you do. If most work is to be done in a studio, a large recorder is preferable. If, however, a lot of work is to be done on location, where the recorder would have to be held or carried by the interviewer, cameraman, or cameraman's assistant, a portable unit would be better. If you do enough different types of work, you may need at least two different types of recorders.

Tape recorders are usually used to record sound on location or in the studio when the sound is to be added to the film later. Recording magnetically first on tape (thereby making all necessary changes and retakes first on the recorder tape) saves a great deal of time and money. Once the final magnetic tape recording is satisfactory, it can be re-recorded onto either an optical sound-track or a magnetic sound-on-film track. The latter, which we discussed above, is by far the easiest for most people to use.

Sound with Motion Pictures: Optical Sound-Tracks

An optical sound-track is a stripe *printed*, the same as a positive picture is printed from a negative, down the side of the film and which reproduces sound by altering a beam of light shining through it (onto a light-sensitive pickup) in the sound head of the projector. In professional film production the optical track is produced first on film that has nothing else (*i.e.*, no picture) on it, and is then printed in combination with the picture frames to produce a "married," or complete sound-and-picture master print.

But why worry about optical sound-tracks at all? For those of you who anticipate a final wide distribution of your film, you have to realize that the optical sound-track is what most theaters and other organizations using sound-on-film utilize. Most large-scale projectors are designed for optical, not magnetic, sound-tracks. It is also more economical to make many duplicates of film that has an optical sound-track. Processing a master, in order to produce numerous prints complete with optical sound-tracks is simpler, faster, automated.

Though optical tracks can be put on other films, it is necessary only to discuss the most proper use of a 16mm optical track. This will tell you enough about the procedure to learn easily, on your own, about any other film you might want to use.

A 16mm stock is needed that is perforated on just one side of the film. The optical sound-track takes up 0.070 to 0.072 inches along the edge of the film not having the sprocket holes. The track may be either variable density or variable area, depending upon the recording equipment. Both are good. I suggest you use whichever your favorite sound studio recommends. They will know what will work best with their equipment and facilities.

When you are matching an optical sound-track to a film you must remember that the sound is 26 frames in advance of the frame to which it is directly related. This is because the sound head — which "reads" the photographically induced wave form on the print of film you are projecting by means of light shining through the sound wave design — is located 26 frames away from the

162

film gate. Therefore, in order that the sound be shown to the sound-producing unit at the same time the picture related to that sound flashes on the screen, this discrepancy must be compensated for. Thus the sound-track on the finished film starts before the first frame, in order that the first sound comes through the speaker at the same time the first frame comes on the screen.

Another thing to remember is that, if your film was shot on negative stock and you are using a print taken directly from that original negative, when you hold the sound-on-film print up to the light with the image right side up and in proper position from left to right, the emulsion of both the picture and the sound-track will face you. In projection, they will both face the projection bulb. However, if the film was shot on reversal stock and the print was made from an intermediate dupe, not directly from the original, the emulsion will be on the other side of the film.

The important point is that when ordering optical sound-track from a 16mm recording studio, you must specify whether the original film was negative or reversal stock, as this affects the location of the optical track.

Just what is the "optical track"? It starts out as a sound negative, recorded down one edge of a separate length of 16mm film, which has nothing at all in the picture area. Later, this sound negative is printed onto the same film, as a positive, in the final film, alongside the pictures. The sound camera that records the optical track may be adjusted to run forward or backward, depending upon whether the final print will have the emulsion toward or away from the projector lens. This is why you must tell the recording studio whether the original film was negative or reversal.

When you are using professionally recorded records or tapes for background you must be sure that you pay the required royalty and make proper arrangements to use copyrighted music, especially if your final product is to be used commercially. Some recordings are royalty-free. There are even organizations that have all sorts of recordings, including sound effects, precisely for the purpose of inclusion in films.

You may fade in, fade out, and mix various sounds and music by using two or more record or tape players. As long as you manipulate the volume controls properly, you should have no problem. Sometimes you may have to make a master tape first, in which you have introduced various effects and music at exactly the right intervals. You can then play this as background for the commentary. In this way you will not be trying to sync. sound effects, music background, and voice all at the same time.

Again, I wish to point out that if you have timed each scene and made a note as to type of music and sound you wish at each timed section of film, you can time recordings to see if they can be synchronized properly with the film.

Here is a simple guide to procedure for preparing sound-on-film:

1. Rough-edit the film.
2. Rough-draft the commentary.
3. Read the commentary aloud, and clearly mark the point before or after the commentary stops that the section of film related to the commentary ran out. Note: If you know the actual footage lengths of each area of film, you can with a stop-watch determine approximately whether they are too short or too long.

4.   Rewrite the commentary, and recheck editing of the movie.

5.   Select music and sound effects, if they are going to be used. (This is the final step for home and other non-professional films.)

6.   Record the commentary while playing the prepared tape of music and sound effects mixed; or if recording the whole thing at once, play recordings while the picture is projected and while record background and voice commentary are played and spoken.

When you are going to make a number of copies of the film, include the following steps:

7.   Prepare the music and effects on separate magnetic tapes.

8.   Prepare a master tape by mixing the commentary (Step 6) with the tape or tapes from Step 7.

9.   Record the master tape to the magnetic strip. When a number of copies are required, each copy will require individual treatment — one of the drawbacks to using magnetic, instead of optical, track. (This is the final step if you are using magnetic sound-track.)

If using 16mm optical track, the following Step 9 would be substituted for the above Step 9:

9.   Record the master tape onto an optical track.

10.   Match the optical track to the picture film by running both optical track and the picture film through a film synchronizer or counter.

11.   Cut the picture film and the sound-track to match all final editing and each other.

12.   Have the married master, or masters, made so that all duplicates will be made of sound and picture simultaneously and automatically, through the photographic optical printing of both picture and track. This is the advantage of the optical track when many copies are needed.

You will, of course, refine the foregoing procedure. These steps are only intended as a rough guide.

If you are going to get into direct sound-recording, that is, picture with sound in perfect synchronization, you really will have to explore further than this book can take you. There are many books, I'm sure, that go into this in detail. I am also sure there are good courses in this field. If you are going to attempt to do anything as advanced as this, I suggest that you hire people who are professionals and rent the equipment necessary to do it right. You get into all sorts of problems once you involve yourself with "lip sync." (synchronization of lips with words) and other sounds that must be exactly synchronized with action. The only exception to this, and the only way in which perfectly synchronized sound may be achieved is by means of videotape (see the chapter on videotape).

With the new magnetic-stripe sound recording projectors, it may be possible to synchronize even lip movements if you are careful enough. The film could be projected and the actors could say their lines in near-perfect sync. with the pictures. It would not be easy, but if mistakes are made, the wonderful flexibility of the magnetic stripe allows you to go back and re-record right over the error. One method you can try is to splice a scene or two (say 3 or 4 feet) into a circular loop (attaching the head of the first scene to the tail of the last scene). Then have the actors (really "readers"), scripts in lap, watch the lip movements of the characters on screen 2 or 3 times as the film loop keeps running through the projector. When the readers think they have their timing down, you can record. Have them go over it as many times as necessary to get it right. In this way, all you have to do is stop the projector whenever you are satisfied with a "take" — all the previous takes will have been erased.

The Value of Sound

There is no question that sound does much for any pictorial presentation. You are missing a great deal if you do not add sound to yours, whether it is for professional, educational, business, or home use. There are many basic rules of application, but in the beginning it really is a matter of using your head. You would not use a polka as background music for two chess players any more than you would use a waltz for musical background in a prizefight (I mean a *good* prizefight)! The tempo and subject of the film itself determine how your musical background should contribute to the pace.

Even the way the commentary is spoken should be in keeping with the mood of the subject matter and the tempo of the scene lengths. Can you imagine anyone using either the pace or the volume of voice connected with auctioneering to do a commntary on an important golf match; or the whisper of the golf commentator to do a commentary on a horse race? You just don't put horse collars on French Poodles! Sound must not only be in the right place at the right time, it must also be the right kind of sound. Tempo, volume, and mood, everything about the sound you use is part of the fabric of your visual presentation. It must contribute to what the film is presenting and to the manner in which you are presenting the subject matter. Sound must not make the presentation "go bump." It must contribute materially to the flow and artistry; it must dovetail with the nature of the subject and the technique of the camera work.

You are going to find tremendous satisfaction in successfully interweaving sound with visual presentation of any kind. You are really going to enjoy what essentially is quite hard work. The proper accomplishment of this hard task is what sets you and your visual presentation above many others and gives it an undeniable mark of achievement and professionalism.

9

Photography's Seven League Boots: The Telephoto Zoom Lens

There is certainly nothing more fantastic, more excitingly magical than the telephoto zoom lenses that are used so often by today's still, motion-picture, and television cameramen! Here is magic of the most practical and helpful sort, magic with which to conquer distance at the turn of a lens! Rotate the zoom control a few inches and you are able, optically, to stride toward the subject over a matter of miles! These are truly photography's "seven league boots."

The telephoto lenses you see illustrated are the largest and bulkiest since they are being used with a 35mm camera; to obtain the same magnification with either 16mm or videotape, you would be able to use considerably more compact telephoto zoom lenses. In 8mm you would, of course, have the most compact, lightest lenses to do a similar job since you are magnifying for the smallest picture area in a camera whose normal focal-length lens is considerably shorter than the normal focal-length lens for 16mm and 35mm. (A normal lens for 35mm cameras is about 50mm, for 16mm and videotape about 25mm, and for Super 8mm about 13mm). Please note the direct ratios that exist between film size and focal length:

$$\frac{35\text{mm (film size)}}{50\text{mm (focal length)}} \quad : \quad \frac{16\text{mm (film size)}}{25\text{mm (focal length)}} \quad : \quad \frac{\text{Super 8mm (film size)}}{12\text{mm (focal length)}}$$

Thus a 4″ x 5″ film size camera (normal lens about 127mm) would require a longer, bulkier, heavier telephoto lens than a 2¼″ x 2¼″ film size (normal lens about 83mm), and so on.

I do think it important to pause and substantiate the foregoing remark about picture quality. In Fig. 9-1, you see the Canon Pellix with a Canon telephoto

Fig. 9-1

zoom lens (PL). This lens, with a 55mm-to-135mm zoom capability, is just 5mm longer at minimum setting than the "normal" focal-length lens for 35mm still cameras. If you can afford only one lens for this camera, you might do well to skip the ordinary 50mm lens and buy only the 55mm-to-135mm zoom lens. Note that the lens, not the camera, is fastened to the Quick-Set tripod head (the lens weighs more than the camera).

Next, take a look at Figs. 9-2a, 9-2b, and 9-2c. Each of these scenes was shot with a different size camera. All three cameras had top-quality lenses, and each, in its own field, represented a standard of high quality comparable to the others. These cameras were: a 4″ x 5″, a 2¼″ x 2¼″ twin-lens reflex, and my 35mm Canon with the 85mm-to-300mm telephoto zoom lens set at its minimum, 85mm focal length. The 4″ x 5″ with its normal lens was working at a 127mm focal length; the 2¼″ x 2¼″ with its normal lens was shooting at an 83mm focal length; and the 35mm Canon with the zoom lens set at 85mm focal length was working at a focal length almost the same as the 2¼″ x 2¼″ but greater than normal for 35mm cameras. One would suppose that the 35mm shot would be taken at a disadvantage (since the lens was already magnifying the image and enlarging it through a focal length of 85mm, which is 35mm beyond its normal 50mm focal length). Before I tell you which photograph was taken by which camera, be a sport — make an honest guess as to which picture was made with which camera. These pictures were all made on the same day, within minutes of each other, by the same cameraman, without filters, and utilizing the same "proper" exposure as determined by the same Weston exposure meter. Naturally, the cameras were set up at about the same spot. The 2¼″ x 2¼″ shot had to be altered because of its shape, and the 35mm shot had to be enlarged because of its size, in order to make a print comparable to the contact print taken with the 4″ x 5″. However, each of the negatives was printed to show the full width of the negative as it actually existed so that you could see camera coverage, from side to side, of an area such as a city. Remember, in asking you

167

Fig. 9-2a

Fig. 9-2b

to guess which camera produced which picture, we are discussing picture quality and sharpness. So, in your answer, make your guess relate to picture clarity.

Fig. 9-2c

If you guessed that Fig. 9-2a was taken by the 35mm, Fig. 9-2b by the 2¼" x 2¼", and Fig. 9-2c by the 4" x 5", you would be joined by the vast majority of 4" x 5" professional photographers and probably by the majority of just plain logical guessers who were relating their answer, as requested, to picture clarity. Meaning nothing personal (and certainly no offense), you would also be all wet! Here is the actual line-up: Fig. 9-2a was taken by the 4" x 5", Fig. 9-2b by the 2¼" x 2¼" (well, you got that one right, at least), and Fig. 9-2c by the 35mm Canon Pellix with the zoom lens at the 85mm setting! Almost makes one feel like going to bed without any supper, doesn't it? Well, don't feel too bad. A little while ago, before my conversion to the exceptional capabilities of such 35mm equipment, I would have been making the same mistake.

How is such a thing possible, let alone believable? The first factor that contributes to making a still picture grainy and less clear (when a positive print is made from the negative) is the fact that many people use high-speed films. These are grainier, and the silver deposits on the negatives are not as fine. Instead, I use Eastman Kodak Panatomic-X, which is about the same speed as my Super 8mm color film. Slow-speed color film has a fine grain; Panatomic-X also has fine grain. So I started out by doing the obvious: I used fine-grain film capable of a similar quality of reproduction as fine-grain color film. Thus my black-and-white picture shot on Panatomic-X did not suffer graininess when it was projected in the enlarger. I just gave the 35mm an equal chance in the simple mechanics of reproduction.

It is my theory that the exceptional clarity of the 35mm picture shot through a zoom lens is also due to a "compaction" of image light rays and an exclusion of light reflection from the surrounding area. After all, the quality of all the lenses employed is topnotch. The 85mm-to-300mm telephoto zoom lens, set at its minimum focal length, was 35mm longer than "normal" (50mm would be normal) for the 35mm camera. Thus the field of view was contracted, less area was photographed, and the scene was magnified so that it would fill the same 35mm negative. I think this tightening of borders results in a little more crisp rendition of image. This may seem strange to many of you because we used to worry about a flattening of image when we used an ordinary telephoto lens instead of the normal focal-length lens for the same camera. With a 50mm lens on a 35mm camera you would have a 46-degree angle of view. With the 85mm setting on the 85mm-to-130mm telephoto zoom on the 35mm, the angle of view is cut down to only 29 degrees! It is my opinion that this compaction of the field of view contributes considerably to snapping up the image rendition. Let's not get too deeply into the theory of the matter. The point is proven by Figs. 9-2a, 9-2b, and 9-2c; with a fine telephoto zoom lens you are certainly not going to lose picture quality! And you might even be able to pick up the scene rendition.

The tremendous advantage of a telephoto zoom is that it can do the work of a whole group of lenses with fixed focal lengths. The zoom lens can vary its focal length; such a lens, mechanically, is constructed of parts and optics that move and realign themselves as you rotate the focal-length setting ring on the lens. Thus, while you are standing at one spot, simply by turning the setting ring and rotating the lens so that it moves back toward or out away from the camera, the focal length of the lens may be changed so that you can be optically as close to or as far from the subject as you desire. There are many times when you may wish to shoot a subject without getting too close. Children at play are often far more natural when you are not right on top of them trying to get your close-ups. With a telephoto zoom lens you can be as close or far as you wish, you can compose your scene accurately, and you can still stay far enough away from the subject so that he is either not aware that you are actually shooting him or will be more relaxed because the camera is not glistening and gleaming just a couple of feet away.

There are times when you just won't want to get too close to the subject. Consider the huge gorillas in the series of scenes in Fig. 9-3, and you will see what can be accomplished in the form of interesting portraiture of animal, or human, activity. What do I mean, "or human"? I'm not taking sides on the Darwinian controversy, but both animal and human (especially children's) behavior patterns in play, sports, gardening, and so on, are quite often repetitious. To capture the activity best, you must stay at a distance and not interrupt the subject's train of thought so that the activity goes on naturally.

To shoot Fig. 9-3, I had to surmount a number of problems. The pictures are all taken of a jumbo-size gorilla in the Bronx Zoo in New York City. I had no intention of sticking my camera within arm's reach of this people-cruncher even if I could have gotten close to him. However, the zoo officials had thoughtfully designed his outdoor habitat so a deep ditch-type area lay between the gorilla and the sightseers. It was impossible to get close enough to procure decent shots with any normal lens. This impossibility was further compounded by the fact that there were youngsters with balloons, adults with cameras, baby carriages, and all manner of abstractions clustered at the fence, which was

Fig. 9-3

closest to the separation ditch and the point at which one normally would have had to position himself in order to get the best shot possible with any normal focal-length lens on any camera. As I have indicated, the best I could do from this distance would have been unacceptable by professional standards and disappointing by any other. Even from such a hard-fought vantage point, the results would be miserable!

As you can see, by using the 55mm-to-125mm telephoto zoom lens on my Canon 35mm camera, I donned my seven-league boots, put on my cloak of invisibility (positioned myself almost on top of the beast without the watching people, or the gorilla, realizing how "close," photographically, I had gotten); failure was changed to success, frustration to complete satisfaction. Because of this wondrous lens I was also able to climb up on some steps, quietly set up my tripod and camera, and click off the poses I wanted. I was unhampered by lollypops, balloons, people, and babies. On these steps I had better elevation, could easily shoot over the bobbing heads of those jammed around the fence, and consequently my camera did not have its view blocked and was not jostled just at the wrong moment. The telephoto zoom allowed me to compose the shots exactly as I wished, all from one position.

In Fig. 9-4, you will see an equally important problem overcome. You can see, in Fig. 9-4a, that the deer are beginning to notice me and my camera, so this was about as close as I was going to get without resorting to luring the animals with feed and generally disrupting their natural daily pursuits. At this distance I could not expose, mainly for the shade, as the foreground took up almost half of the picture area and was all in bright sunlight; exposing for the shade would have resulted in a washed-out foreground that would have ruined the scene. As it was, you can see that I was forced to overexpose slightly the closest section of the foreground at the bottom of this picture.

The leader of the herd still watches as I turn my 55mm-to-135mm telephoto zoom into place on my Canon 35mm camera. Now I could afford to expose more for the shadow area; look at the difference in actual subject rendition! You can really look into the shade and see what is there; the subject itself is perfectly exposed and the detail is splendid.

Next I backed away a little, feigning disinterest, with my back to the deer. By the time I turned the lens toward my subject, he was still keeping a weather eye on me but was proceeding more naturally to collect one of the does which had had the audacity to wander from his herd. Figure 9-4c caught him as he moseyed down the trail to get her back.

By rotating the telephoto zoom a little I was able to move in for a study of this deer as he waited for his doe to climb back up a hill. He had just finished scolding her with what I'm sure was some very profane deer language.

In Fig. 9-4d, the deer has a self-satisfied look on his face as his demands are respected and the doe comes up the hill. By rotating the zoom lens to its maximum 135mm setting, I was able to get an excellent close shot. The deer is still berating the doe as he herds her toward the fold. It looks like the doe is muttering some sarcastic retort under her breath as she heads back into the herd.

This whole intimate series would have been impossible with normal focal-length lenses; I'm sure you know this, so it is not necessary to belabor the point.

Fig. 9-4a

Fig. 9-4b

Fig. 9-4c

Fig. 9-4d

Fig. 9-4e

Fig. 9-4f

Camera and Lens Technique

In my *Handbook of Basic Motion Picture Techniques,* the first chapter explains that *panning* is the primary obstacle between the cameraman and good motion-picture making. Panning is the moving of the motion-picture camera while it is running to view area after area of a scene. Its purpose is to film a panoramic view. For the beginner, panning almost always results in an abortive attempt that kills enjoyment and communication. The amateur motion-picture cameraman, in panning, creates a jumble of off-balance, cockeyed, crooked, pictorially poor individual frames. Remember this: Motion-picture film consists of a series of still pictures, one below the other, shot in rapid sequence. If you hold a strip of movie film up to the light you will see, one below the other, still picture below still picture, each one shot just a fraction of a second after the preceding one. What a motion-picture camera really is is a photographic machine gun. When all these still pictures are projected through a movie projector — which is just a rapid-fire still-picture projector — the still pictures come on so fast, one after the other, that the viewer thinks he is seeing *one* scene, and the slight advancement of action in each of the still pictures creates the illusion of motion and continuity. Unless you are trying for a special effect involving a certain amount of purposeful distortion, do not use a pan scene to "get in" a wide area; remember that each little frame on your movie film should be a good, well-composed, still picture, which it cannot be if your camera is moving while you are shooting.

If you must have an exceptionally wide view of an area, the proper way to get it is to use a wide-angle lens so that a panoramic still shot can be made without moving the camera while shooting. *Always use a tripod;* failing this, find some solid support. While I prefer to have my camera on a good solid tripod with almost unlimited adjustability (such as with the Quick-Set Hi-Boy tripod), it is often useful to have a smaller tripod, too. If you must travel light, you can always manage to take along one of the sturdier table-top tripods. Some of these even have a crank-up central shaft (like the Quick-Set) and can be opened to a 6- to 7-foot height. You are only kidding yourself and robbing your pictures (still, motion, or video) of that additional touch of professionalism if you do not use a tripod. Frankly, after over a quarter of a century, I find that I am automatically more professional, compose my pictures more carefully, and give more thought to the shot if I use a tripod. It is not just a matter of steadiness, so that motion pictures do not bob and weave on the screen in projection. It is a matter of being mentally committed to the idea that the scene is worth devoting some time to and that you are setting up to give it sufficient thought. When the camera is hand-held, there is an overwhelming tendency *not* to see details, *not* to make sure you have the right angle, *not* to compose carefully. When the camera is held rock-steady the photographer can more easily search every area of the picture. He will not see just the generalization of a scene, but every detail in the background, foreground, and the corners.

Not only is it wrong to pan a motion picture or TV camera while shooting (except for special effects) in an attempt to show everything you wish to get in; it is an unnatural way to try to simulate vision. Think about it. When you look at a distant building, you see the building and you get an impression of its surroundings, but you do not see too much too clearly. In a way, your eyes have their own special zoom apparatus, more highly refined than that of any lens. Your mind can focus your eyes on a small area of interest; even from a great distance. While this area is not magnified (we use binoculars to move in closer), the less interesting part of a scene is subordinated by soft focus. A camera lens is sharp across the whole of the scene (except when you purposely set it to have a different or special effect), seeing anything within a certain plane. These differences between the vision of the camera and that of the human eye present problems for the cameraman. Selective focus and panning are inadequate solutions. Although they appear to simulate what the human eye

Fig. 9-5a

Fig. 9-5b

Fig. 9-5c

Fig. 9-5d

Fig. 9-5e

Fig. 9-5f

Fig. 9-5g

does under similar conditions, they are disruptive effects, when projected. The audience's awareness of the effect — and, therefore, of the camera — interrupts their continuity of concentration. To make the audience unaware of the camera's operations, it is necessary to resort to techniques that give an effect of human mind and eye processes without copying them directly.

The simplest and most effective technique that allows you to cope with this disparity between human and camera vision is the well-established shot breakdown of long shot, medium shot, and close-up. With a normal fixed focal-length lens (not a telephoto zoom), the technique would be to take three shots, at three distances from the subject: one from far away, one from a halfway point, and one from close up. In this way you would literally take the audience by the hand and walk them in to the point of major interest. With the zoom lens, you can take the three shots without ever moving.

In Fig. 9-5, there are six scenes, just a few of the many that can be made from the same spot with a telephoto zoom lens. You would usually not need all of the scenes shown, but I have included them to help you to realize the technique of properly utilizing the wonderful magic of the telephoto zoom. The secret of success is that you would normally not shoot the first scene until you had decided what the last scene was going to feature. When you shoot Fig. 9-5a, you should have already decided that the last scene will look exactly like Fig. 9-5f.

All of the scenes in Fig. 9-5 were made with the Canon Pellix 85mm-to-300mm telephoto zoom lens from the same spot, on the west shore of the Hudson River. You could open with either Fig. 9-5a or 9-5b, but I would suggest a shot like Fig. 9-5a because it establishes the Jersey shore. The dark dock running from the left-hand corner of the picture serves as a huge pointer to direct attention toward the two boats in New York harbor. Figure 9-5b would not be used if your final close-up were going to be the two pleasure boats in New York harbor. Figure 9-5b features the Empire State Building and the boats are subordinated to it in this scene. This directs the audience's attention toward the subject that you have chosen to zero in on.

Figure 9-5d would be the next shot, as it shows an area around the main subject in such a way that there can be no mistake as to the subject's surroundings and location in those surroundings. Figure 9-5c did not show enough more than Fig. 9-5d to justify its inclusion, and Fig. 9-5b was a weaker shot than Fig. 9-5a, from a compositional standpoint. Thus Figs. 9-5b and 9-5c are not necessary and would tend to detract from the impact of the other scenes. On the other hand, Fig. 9-5d does show adequate surrounding area while still, obviously, featuring the two pleasure boats at dock.

Figure 9-5e would be omitted in favor of Fig. 9-5f. Figure 9-5e slices off the spire of the Chrysler Building, and does nothing that Figs. 9-5d and 9-5f do not do better.

Thus, through the process of selection, we have:

Long shot: Figure 9-5a, to establish general location and orient the audience. Our subject is boats in the Hudson River of New York.

Medium shot: Figure 9-5d, to narrow down and concentrate attention.

Close-up: Figure 9-5f, to show most intimately the subject as much as distance and lens capability allowed. In this scene the telephoto zoom was set at its maximum focal length — 300mm. At this setting, it magnified the subject as much as it could.

I'm sure I don't have to tell you how difficult and time-consuming it would have been to get such shots without a telephoto lens setup of some sort.

Of course, if you visit New York City, you must go to the top of the Empire State Building. With this in mind, you ought to make a good transitional shot. While you are still at the location from which you shot the pictures of the pleasure boats, one more scene should be shot quite similar to Fig. 9-5d but with the tripod head loose as you start the scene so that you are ready to zoom in on the Chrysler Building. Let the camera run about one second before starting to zoom in. Then, as you zoom, tilt your camera slowly and turn it so that you keep the Chrysler Building centered in your viewfinder. When the area is narrowed-down enough so that the boats no longer appear in the scene and the Chrysler Building is fairly prominent, you have introduced your next scene and you are ready to go to the Empire State Building.

Once you are atop the Empire State Building, one of the world's greatest metropolises stretches out in every direction before you. While you may make many scenes in many directions, do these only after you have gotten what you specifically came to shoot — those scenes in which the Chrysler Building is featured. Again, the illustration is comprised of scenes made with the 85mm-to-300mm telephoto zoom lens on the Canon Pellix 35mm camera. Figures 9-6a-6g were made at the following zoom positions: Fig. 9-6a, 85mm; Fig. 9-6b, 100mm; Fig. 9-6c, 135mm; Fig. 9-6d, 160mm; Fig. 9-6e, 200mm; Fig. 9-6f, 250mm; and Fig. 9-6g, 300mm. Again, three scenes will suffice quite nicely; these could be the following:

Long shot: Figure 9-6b was used because Fig. 9-6a is too weak. The Pan Am Building competes too strongly with our subject in Fig. 9-6a. In Fig. 9-6b, the Pan Am Building still attracts attention but the Chrysler Building, in a more central position, is really the focal point.

Medium shot: Figure 9-6e was chosen because Fig. 9-6c puts the Pan Am Building on an almost equal footing of importance with the Chrysler Building. Figure 9-6d would have been an acceptable scene, but it is not nearly as forceful as Fig. 9-6e. In Fig. 9-6e the Chrysler Building has been shown in a slightly less prominent area of the scene, left of center, so that the bridge and the industrial area begin to take on interest.

Close-up: Figure 9-6g shows the Chrysler Building in such a way that its most interesting section may be studied in detail. Still the audience is invited to look beyond the building into the vast areas it so easily dominates. Figure 9-6f places the Chrysler Building too much in the center of things where it cuts the panorama in half. Figure 9-6g, closing in on the most interesting detail of the building, also allows it to become foreground area once the viewer looks beyond into the surrounding area.

As for Fig. 9-7, you must remember that you do not shoot close-ups just to be as close as you can get, or long shots just to see as much as possible. Good technique and utilization of equipment demand qualities that cannot be taught — common sense and creativity. The employment of certain principles in a

Fig. 9-6a

Fig. 9-6b

Fig. 9-6c

Fig. 9-6d

Fig. 9-6e

Fig. 9-6f

Fig. 9-6g

178

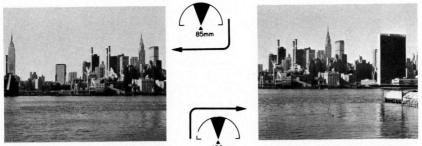

Fig. 9-7a

Fig. 9-7b

Fig. 9-7c

Fig. 9-7d

Fig. 9-7e

Fig. 9-7f

Fig. 9-7g

wise and effective manner will result in your creativity being realized to its fullest. In this series, taking into consideration the other scenes we have made from other locations and our general treatment, we would employ the following shots:

Long shot: Figure 9-7a shows the Empire State Building, from which we had made our shots of the Chrysler Building, and the location and proportions of these two outstanding giants in relation to each other.

Long shot: In Fig. 9-7b, common sense dictated a variance from the usual formula of long shot, medium shot, and close-up. We shot Fig. 9-7a with the telephoto zoom set at 85mm, but we could not get the Empire State Building, the Chrysler Building, and the United Nations Building all in the same picture without framing everything too tightly and having too many important and dominating objects all fighting for attention at the same time. This time we excluded the Empire State Building, and changed to the 100mm zoom position. Though the United Nations Building is a very strong dark mass, its prominence is controlled by placing it at the right of the frame and having the Chrysler Building almost at dead center. This makes the Chrysler Building the bull's-eye object.

Medium close-up: Figure 9-7d is the last scene in which we can achieve good composition with the camera at this location. There is no question that the Chrysler Building is the center of interest. We used the 160mm setting and made this our concluding scene. Figures 9-7e, 9-7f, and 9-7g did not show us anything we had not seen in the shots taken from the Empire State Building and were, because of the location of the Pan Am Building compositionally poor. We already have ample intimate shots in Fig. 9-6 to give us an excellent close-up view of the Chrysler Building without having to sacrifice good composition. The close-ups we could have gotten from the east side of Manhattan would not have added anything to our overall story and would not have given us any new information.

With the 85mm-to-300mm telephoto zoom lens it would be possible to shoot sufficient coverage of the New York skyline in just one day. I would suggest shooting the east side areas in the morning from the east bank of the East River — from the southern Queens—northern Brooklyn area. In the morning, the sun should be shining full upon the east side of the buildings in Manhattan. Then you can go to the Empire State Building and get shots such as you saw in Fig. 9-6 from about 1 until 3 P.M. Even if you got to the top of the Empire State Building earlier, it would do no harm. You could make plenty of other scenes while waiting for the best light on the main areas. The important thing would be for you to leave there no later than 3 P.M. in the winter and no later than 4 P.M. in summer; this would allow you enough time to beat the commuter traffic if it were a weekday and get across the Hudson to a vantage point on the west bank of the Hudson River (in New Jersey) so that you could shoot across the river at the west side of New York City while it was well illuminated by the afternoon sun.

You can save a lot of running back and forth when you are visiting a place by simply getting a good map of the area and checking to see what areas face which direction. All you have to do, then, is figure from the map how you

180

Fig. 9-8a   Fig. 9-8b

want the sun at the time you are shooting any particular subject and plan. Once you know the north, south, east, and west sides of the subject, planning when to shoot is easy.

In Fig. 9-7, I have included some rough sketches to show you just what has happened in each setting of the telephoto zoom lens. The blacked-in area the shape of a piece of pie indicates, in each sketch, the angle of view that the lens covered at each setting. At the 85mm setting, the lens had a field of view of 29 degrees. At the 100mm setting, the field of view was about 24 degrees; at 135mm about 18 degrees; at 200mm about 12 degrees; at 250mm about 10 degrees; and at 300 only about 8 degrees. You can readily see that, as you bring the subject closer, optically, you narrow the field of view considerably.

When you are on a trip or pressed for time, for other reasons the telephoto lens is a godsend; and the telephoto zoom is pure magic. How often have you wanted to get a shot of birds and were able to sneak up almost close enough — but not quite? Again, when you are vacationing, you may often like a particular shot, but you just don't want to make a project of getting it. Anyone knows that if you lay out some bait-fish, you will have no trouble getting sea gulls, for example, to come close to you. I recommend doing this when you want to make extensive, serious studies of them. However, with the telephoto zoom you can "stride in" to get some pretty good close-ups without a lot of time and effort.

Figure 9-8a is a shot made with my telephoto zoom set at 85mm; while this may be okay as a panoramic long shot, it fails to enlarge the birds enough to mean anything. Figure 9-8b, however, was made with the telephoto zoom set at 300mm. In either slide, videotape, or motion-picture projection, Fig. 9-8b would be quite effective. The lead bird evidently gave quite a kick while flapping its wings and became airborne almost instantly. This picture, shot at about 1/500 sec., almost stopped the wing movement completely on the lead bird and did freeze it entirely in the second bird, at right. As I have said, such still pictures make excellent freeze-frames in such things as bird studies, sports, etc., when you want frozen action to appear as sharp as possible. The single frames that you might freeze from normal movie film would be shot at about 1/30 sec. and much of the action will not have this needle-sharpness. In such cases the still camera, with its ultra-high speeds — my Canon has a focal-plane shutter that goes as fast as 1/1000 sec. — and the telephoto zoom can contribute quite a bit to movies or videotape.

The zoom lens on my Bell & Howell Super 8mm camera runs from 9mm (wide-angle) to 45mm (telephoto). Thus I could make these gulls fill the frame almost as much as I could with the still camera; but in each individual frame I would not have the high shutter speed of the still camera.

Many interesting scenes of the gulls in flight could be made with the movie camera alone, and some great use could be made of slow motion. The camera would run the film faster and boost the individual frame exposure from 1/30 sec. (at 16 frames per second) to 1/60 sec. (at 36 fps). You would not want to shoot all the in-flight scenes in slow motion, as such scenes would become boring. Slow motion is a special effect and, like any other, it too should be used sparingly.

There are a few drawbacks that you must bear in mind when using a telephoto lens, zoom or otherwise. As you narrow down the angle of vision and magnify to a greater and greater extent a smaller segment of your scene, you are also magnifying and accentuating camera shake. That is, as you increase focal length, you are not only enlarging the scene, but also the effects of camera movement. So, even if you are using a still camera, put it on a tripod, especially if you are shooting at shutter speeds below 1/50 sec.

The second drawback related to greater focal length is that as the focal length gets longer, the depth of field grows shorter; conversely, as the focal length shrinks, the depth of field increases. Be sure to obtain related depth-of-field charts from the manufacturer of your lens. In still work, if you must hand-hold while shooting with a telephoto lens, try to shoot at the higher shutter speeds (1/250 sec. or higher) to help minimize any possible movement of the camera during exposure.

You also want to remember that when you are shooting long shots, medium shots, and close-ups with a telephoto, you should move your tripod around a little between shots. Move slightly to one side, elevate it, change angle horizontally and vertically, so that all the shots will not be made from exactly the same angle. Sometimes you will not be able to do much of this, but when you can it provides pleasing variety. It is more interesting to see scenes that differ not only in distance from the subject but also in angle of view.

I have but scratched the surface of zoom possibilities. You have all viewed movie scenes of football games in which the camera took you in close to the action while it was occurring; you had the feeling you were riding a magic carpet right down onto the playing field. The cameraman rotated his zoom lens while the camera was running so you saw the scene being magnified as the focal length of the zoom lens was increased. This is very effective, but don't overdo it. A little goes a long way!

In still photography, you may get special effects with lights at night by using a time exposure and, while the shutter is open, rotating the zoom lens so that the focal length of the lens changes while the time exposure is being made. I suggest that you experiment with this special effect, but, again, use it very sparingly.

Whether the telephoto zoom lens is used for practical or special-effect purposes, it is undoubtedly one of the most valuable and exciting accessories to photography. Don't spoil its tremendous utility by poor, unwise usage. Use your common sense, and this wonderful optical tool will reward you endlessly.

10

Videotape

A most fitting description of videotape would be "instant sound movies." Videotape is to movie-making what the Polaroid camera has been to the still camera field. This is, of course, a most elementary comparison; in fact, videotape equipment has many more advantages. With videotape, you see exactly what your camera is going to record and just how it will expose it, prior to and during the exposure. You can use the same "film" (tape) over again (provided you do not wish a permanent record of what you have shot). And you can record sound right along with picture.

Many additional virtues of videotape will become self-evident as we get deeper into this chapter. We must remember, too, that nothing can be all things to all men. No single type of equipment can best fill the needs in any field. The Polaroid camera did not replace the regular still camera; I am sure the videotape camera will not replace the regular motion-picture camera. Both have a rightful and important place in the world of photography; each serves best different areas of that world. In some cases both videotape and ordinary cameras are used, in combination with each other. For example, there are times when a TV program will use live action, taped sequences, film segments, and still pictures in the same program. But if you are interested in any type of photography, I think you will find an exploration of videotape relevant, stimulating, and fun.

Those of you who already have videotape equipment or later go on to rent or buy it will realize that videotaping involves the use of a camera. Since this camera records action, the technique of using a videotape camera is in many ways similar to the technique of using a motion-picture camera. Consequently, what you know about the esthetics of motion-picture work will serve you in good stead with videotape.

Equipment

What precisely is *videotape?* Many of you have a tape recorder of some sort. What serves as "film" for both sound and picture in videotaping looks just like ordinary recording tape, except that it is often as much as four times as wide. Ordinary tape for voice recording only is about one-quarter-inch wide,

Fig. 10-1

Fig. 10-2

Fig. 10-3

Fig. 10-4

whereas the videotape for my Ampex is about one-inch wide, and records picture and voice — picture via the camera, voice via a mike — together. In Fig. 10-1, you see a simple, but complete, videotape setup for taking, monitoring, and playing back videotape. In the illustration, the cameraman is checking a close-up image directly on his monitor. You can use an ordinary TV set as a monitor if you wish. There are three pieces of equipment in the setup: an Ampex videotape camera, with a microphone that can be used either with the camera or can be plugged directly into the recorder, an Ampex videotape recorder (left foreground) ; and a TV set for use as a monitor and playback screen.

With the Ampex recorder, you may also play back compatible tapes made commercially or by you, just as an ordinary tape recorder not only allows you to make tapes, but also play back the tapes you have made or bought.

Educational Uses

I am sure most of you have seen instant replays of football plays and other sports action on TV. Ampex videotape equipment allows you to make similar instant playbacks at home, in school, in industry — almost anywhere where there is a source of electricity to run the camera, recorder, and TV monitor. In Fig. 10-1, an operatic teacher is getting ready to use his Ampex equipment to shoot one of his opera students performing. Not only can the voice be played back so that the singer may hear how others will hear her, but also her motion pictures will be played back, so that her delivery will be shown; she will see herself almost exactly as others see her. The usefulness of such tools, in teaching acting and singing, cannot be overestimated. The fact, too, that the recorded voice and picture can be instantly played back, while the student still recalls freshly how and what he thought he was doing, is almost self-corrective.

Still more to the point, from an educational standpoint, some music schools equipped with videotape show pupils videotapes made by professionals. This can be followed by the students' own performances of the same scenes, permitting immediate comparison. The student may promptly hold the yardstick of professional performance up to his own effort, viewing and hearing them both through the same equipment.

In Fig. 10-2, the recorder is still in the left foreground, but the monitor and camera have been moved to a more distant location. This underlines an important point — that you should often use your videotape camera as though you were actually making a small motion-picture production. While the camera should be moved in for close-ups, it should also be moved *back* for long shots. In this way the student (of opera or acting) will get used to the realization that the whole body is involved, from head to toe — singing and acting do not exist only in close-ups.

So that the teacher or director may concentrate on instruction, I suggest that someone else operate the camera and still another helper operate the recorder. I also suggest that the monitor, showing the scene as it is being taped, be placed to one side and angled, if possible, so that both the cameraman and the instructor may easily check the action. The recorder operator should also be able to see the monitor, so that when it comes time to play back he will be able to see the playback as well as hear it. When placing the monitor and recorder, consideration should also be given to the cameraman's freedom of movement. When the camera is moved back for a long shot or in for a close-up, the cameraman should be able to dolly freely and easily, with minimum loss of time and without tripping over the wire running between the camera and the recorder. Basic videotape cameras are very light. Moving one and its tripod takes no more effort than moving an ordinary Super 8mm or 16mm camera and its tripod — provided the monitor, recorder, and camera are arranged so that the wire from the camera to the recorder will reach long-shot and close-up extremes without becoming disconnected. In some cases, in which there is a long distance between long-shot and close-up camera positions, it is wise to provide a sufficient extra amount of cable. I suggest obtaining this from the maker of your equipment so that the additional cable will match all the wires in the original length of cable.

The instructor in Fig. 10-2 is doing another very intelligent thing. He is putting the actors through a dry run — televised but not taped — before actually videotaping them. He coaches them in the actions and delivery until he is satisfied that they have really gotten the idea of what should be done. When the teacher feels the student has mastered proper delivery or, on the other hand, when he feels he cannot get through to a student, the instructor can then videotape.

During dry runs, it is often helpful if the monitor can be seen by the players. This can be accomplished with mirrors if the monitor cannot be positioned so that everyone can see it simultaneously.

Sports Uses

In the field of sports, the advantages of instant playback need no emphasis. For years now, coaches have made films of their own players and their opponents so that every play and movement could be carefully studied. Now it is possible to play back any action instantly, without waiting for film to be processed and returned. This application of videotape to sports is unlimited. Tennis, golf, baseball, hockey, track, football — name a sport and you have named an area in which videotaping is useful.

I'm sure many readers of this book are bowlers. Need I ask you how many nights you have suffered, when in a slump, trying to figure out just exactly what it was you could possibly be doing so differently from the nights on which you bowled so much better? Even though someone, in a kind way, has tried to help, hasn't it been most difficult to follow his advice? On the other hand, you know how easy it is for you to see what another bowler is doing wrong, as you sit back and watch his delivery. Videotape makes it possible for the bowler to see for himself what he is doing wrong — whether he is rushing his approach or is crossing his arm over his body instead of working it in that smooth pendulum motion. Whatever the trouble, the bowler will see himself as others are able to see him — and just seconds after he has thrown the ball! His action can be played and replayed until he is sure he is not mistaken about the fault. In the hands of a professional bowling instructor, of course, videotape equipment becomes just that much more effective. Not only can the instructor point out what the bowler is doing wrong, but corrective measures may also be videotaped and shown to him. Additional videotaping, as the bowler attempts to follow corrective suggestions, can be replayed to the bowler immediately after he has attempted to approach and deliver as instructed. He can instantly view how close his efforts are coming to the advice. Thus, in sports, too, video-taping is the latest, most effective method of complete instruction.

Figure 10-3 shows members of a bowling school in Albany, N.Y., where Ampex videotape equipment is used in instruction. The bowler in the right foreground has just completed a frame of bowling and is now seated with another pupil, listening to the instructor's critique of his actions.

Business Uses

Figure 10-4 shows just one of the many uses of videotape in the business world. At this heavy-machinery rebuilding plant in California, a machine conversion is being videotaped so that it may be replayed to newly hired machinists. By utilizing videotape to illustrate how the work is accomplished by a highly skilled and experienced technician, this firm accomplishes a number of time- and money-saving objectives and presents a singularly perfect and uniform example of instruction.

Once the operation is videotaped, neither the machinery nor the technician has to be tied up for long periods of time to redemonstrate the technique involved in this operation.

Mobility of instruction is unlimited. The videotape may be duplicated and distributed to an organization's branch offices. This picture-and-sound presentation of the operation may be used not only in training but also as a sales aid — say, by demonstrating equipment to prospective clients.

The videotape camera may be moved in for close-ups and ultra-close-ups to show the most intimate detail of any part of the demonstration. Sound, recorded simultaneously on the tape, can further explain these details. The camera can be moved back for long shots and medium shots (to keep the viewer oriented to the general location of the various details). It may be constantly moved in close to details, viewing them from the best possible angle, so the most revealing view can be had by all trainees as the tape is played back on a TV screen. It is no longer necessary to wait until each trainee moves himself to the proper distance and vantage point each time an important action takes place. It is now only necessary to have the camera moved to that vantage point.

Still-framing (freezing the action so it remains stopped) at any vital point is also possible with some videotape equipment. For purposes of standardized presentation, I suggest simply stopping the action at such points and allowing the camera to record the stopped action naturally. Freeze-frame use is best confined to operations in which it is difficult to hold the action still or stop machinery and operation.

The foregoing are just a few instances in which videotaping can perform virtual miracles in effective training and sales presentations. It should also be mentioned that videotape can improve and clarify communications between offices and/or firms having compatible equipment. For instance, suppose a certain piece of machinery needed modification. A sketch could be shown along with the actual part, and both picture and sound could carefully point out each detail of change. This technique could be utilized in making a wooden mock-up, for instance, either to scale or in actual size, so that both picture and sound would relate the most detailed and accurate description of a change or even a new design.

Slides and Films in Videotape

Figure 10-5 indicates the usefulness of slides and motion-picture films in conjunction with videotape. You should have no trouble taking pictures of either slides or motion pictures with videotape equipment, as the lens is always open. Therefore, there can be no danger of the projector and camera being out of synchronization. Since videotape has such a tremendous latitude, both in exposure and contrast, use of projected backgrounds and of other projected scenes becomes highly practical. You must bear in mind, of course, that you must balance the lighting between any projected scene and anything live you may

Fig. 10-5

wish to combine with it. In Fig. 10-5, a model airplane is shown as though it were traveling high above the clouds. It is actually projected on a process screen set in back of the plane. A good lighting balance had to be achieved between the plane in the foreground and the clouds on the process screen behind.

Aside from backgrounds, taping miniature sets, and enhancement of titles, projected images may be used in other exciting ways. The field of special effects is very fertile. For example, you may videotape a projected film first as is, then in reverse. You can have a diver pop up out of the water and back onto the springboard; or in a football scene, you can have a caught pass pop out of the receiver's hands and travel back to the passer. There is no end to the possibilities.

Reverse action may be used seriously, too, for teaching. In coaching a football team, for instance, a videotape can be shown of a player going into a block. This tape can be stopped at any point — say the point of maximum execution — then reversed to show, emphatically, just what he did well or, if he missed the block, exactly where he went wrong.

It is absolutely amazing what a still slide can contribute if inserted as a scene of frozen action in the middle of a motion picture or videotape action sequence. The flight of a sea gull is a dramatic example. To show a gull's flight in detail, you would need an extreme telephoto lens, preferably a telephoto zoom and a very high shutter speed. The videotape equipment can yield a telephoto view, but it cannot give you frozen action of a fast-moving object. Even 64 frames per second, which is the highest speed on most movie cameras today, gives a shutter speed of only 1/120 sec. for each frame. A 35mm still camera, on the other hand, offers many times that shutter speed. My Canon Pellix, with its focal-plane shutter, enables you to shoot at speeds up to 1/1000 sec. With such speeds, you can stop action cold in its tracks. With practice, you can shoot many stills in rapid succession. Even at speeds of 1/500 or 1/250 sec., much action can be frozen, and a dramatic record of the gull's movements can be made. The resulting slides can later be projected and shot with your videotape camera.

Servicing and Technique

For further information concerning videotaping equipment, contact the manufacturers of the various brands. I especially recommend getting in touch with Ampex Corporation, Consumer & Educational Products Division, 2201 Lunt Ave., Elk Grove, Ill. 60007. They have a complete line of videotaping equipment and are unusually helpful and informative. So far, my Ampex equipment has remained quite trouble-free and has required only the reasonable care that any owner might perform. But it is a good idea, before investing in any videotape equipment, to see what repair services are available in your area and to buy your equipment with such exigencies in mind.

I find it a good rule to have my equipment serviced periodically, if only to be checked out by a competent technician equipped with the relevant service information. Such attention will often prolong the life of equipment by many years and will insure top-notch performance during this life. In the long run, it is bound to pay off in both results and savings.

Index

191